CROSS CANADA ADVENTURES

Two Journeys
A Lifetime Apart

Ralph Martin

Blueskies Press

Canada

Copyright © Ralph Martin 2017

Cataloguing data available from Library and Archives Canada

ISBN 978-1-7750554-0-2 (Paperback)

Blueskies Press

1083 Troy Place

Qualicum Beach B.C V9K 2G5

Printed and bound in Canada

For the little red-haired girl.

Table of Contents

FOREWORD

Canada is big. By road it is more than 7,500 kilometres from Vancouver Island to St. John's Newfoundland. If you could drive the same distance west from Victoria you would be in the suburbs of Tokyo and the same trip east from St. John's would land you in the parking lot of the Great Pyramid of Khufu with enough left on the odometer to cruise around Cairo and find a Starbucks.

Canada is a land of big nature: big mountains, big rivers, big prairies, lakes and skies. Big bays, big islands, big rain, trees, and waterfalls. Everything from big oil in Alberta to big tides in the Bay of Fundy and just plain Biggar in Saskatchewan. Canada has all manner of weather, often in the same place at the same time, and Canada has big animals, like moose and bears and bison. Despite being surrounded by so much bigness Canadians are fond of raising monuments and statues that give gigantic dimension to even the small and commonplace. What Canadian hasn't heard of the Vegreville Pysanka, the Wawa Goose, or the Big Fiddle in Sydney? (What Canadian hasn't incorrectly, but understandably, assumed that the Big Fiddle must be in Ottawa?)

Canada is also a land of traditions: Hockey Night in Canada, Kraft Dinner, a new Chia Pet for Granny every Christmas, and Tim-Bits after the kids' (insert sport of your choice) game every Saturday. Traditions change from place to place and from time to time but the one quintessential tradition that touches all Canadians is the road trip. And the grand-daddy of all road trips is the great 7,500-kilometre odyssey from one coast to the other. It's a big trip and while almost all Canadians have done bits and pieces of it in fits and starts few of them make it all the way all at once.

Ralph has done the complete trip, twice over, and here shares his engaging and humorous narrative of both journeys: a newly retired traveller in a camper van criss-crossing the path of his seventeen-year-old backpacking self hitchhiking his way across the country 40-odd years earlier. The places and people, details and insights of the parallel experiences will bring a knowing smile to the face of anyone who has made the same journey and a gentle pang of regret to those who always knew they should have. 7,500 kilometres to the other end of the country and 7,500 kilometres back amounts to more than half way around the world at the 49th parallel. This book will take you both ways twice, put a smile on your face, and save you a ton of gas money, so crack a cold one and hit the road.

Bob Collins

Beyond Hope

I am not yet beyond hope; I am writing this in a campground in Hope, B.C., a place I have always considered to be the edge of the known world. To a westcoaster like me, Hope is the gateway to the rest of Canada. Tomorrow morning my wife and I will be off on our adventure across Canada. We will be definitely beyond Hope.

The first time I went across Canada was many years ago, in 1970, when I hitchhiked alone. Thumbing a ride was a thing young people did back then. Before I left home, my mother warned me that I would surely find myself in bad company: drunkards, drug dealers, lunatics, murderers, and loose women. She was right. The murderer part occurred pretty early on, but before I tell you about the killer I met, I should begin at the beginning…or close to it.

I remember when I decided to go to the east coast. It was because of a hat. I made my decision during a great weekend spent on the west coast of Vancouver Island (the "Island") at Long Beach near Tofino. In those days, it was much harder to get there. The road through the central mountains from Port Alberni was rough gravel and excitingly winding, including a particularly nasty batch of steep switchbacks.

2

I had been out there with two buddies earlier that year escaping a boring day at school at the tail end of winter. My friend had one of those old fastback Volvos that he dearly loved to drive. I had grown up on farm trucks and big old sedans, so was unused to John's road rally car and road rally driving. A couple of times I was more than a little anxious as we raced out to Long Beach, but as soon as I realized I was in good hands, I settled in to enjoy the ride.

The road we had been travelling on was rough, and narrow, and snaked through thick, dark mountain forest for a long enough time for it to begin to feel tiresome and tedious. It was the first time I had been over that particular road and really didn't know what to expect. I was quite unprepared when suddenly we came out of the shadows and found ourselves on a cleared hillside. The bright world had opened in front of us. It was fantastic. The miles of beach and the Pacific Ocean stretched out in front like an awakening. I was absolutely astounded. It is a scene I'll keep forever.

We were so impressed by our visit to the place that a few weeks later, we organized an exodus from school to camp out on the beach. There were piles of driftwood all along sand at the edge of the forest. It was no large task to make a kind of lean-to settlement. We had plenty of polyethylene sheeting and a few tarps, and we staked our claim amongst the other hippies. With plenty of substances to abuse and basic foods like chili and bread, we were ready to party away the weekend.

You could drive on the beach in those days. We found that sitting on a stout canvas tarpaulin pulled behind a VW van made a great ride across the sand. Unfortunately, when driving on the beach, there was a real risk of losing your vehicle if you found a soft spot and the tide came in. I remember two vehicles that had gone to their rest in that sand. The discovery of the first came as a surprise when I heard a strange kabunk noise as my buddy Gord and I walked on the beach.

I said to Gord, "Sand doesn't go *kabunk!*"

I walked back and forth a couple of times to get an exact location and fifteen minutes digging with our hands revealed the top of what we reckoned was a VW bug. No wonder the west coast is called the Graveyard of the Pacific, although I think that name was more for ships than little cars. The second vehicle's end was more dramatic and amusing.

As I said before, in those days you could drive on the beach. It was all kinds of fun. There were lots and lots of young people on the beach driving lots and lots of cars, so it should not come as a big surprise to learn that some of them were drinking beer while they drove. A lot of beer. Enough beer to make a nuisance of themselves and to encourage the local constabulary to bring their police car onto the beach and put an end to the drunk driving.

Now, most of those young people's cars were not expensive. In fact, it was a wonder that some of them even managed to make the drive to the west coast. The one that the police were particularly interested in had no muffler because that bit was probably somewhere on the nasty gravel road from Port Alberni. That car also boasted lots of rust, a missing tail light, dents and scratches, and rough body repairs, resulting in a net value that was probably less than the beer it carried. Quite an audience gathered to watch as the police herded those hooligans to our end of the beach where large rocks blocked any further progress. When the occupants of the car saw that there was no escape those gangsters turned their car in the direction of China. Shouting, "You'll never take this car alive, Coppers!" they drove it straight into the sea until the water was halfway up the doors. They climbed out of the windows and sat on the roof laughing and finishing the last of their beers.

After we enjoyed the car chase and the antics of the gangsters, things quieted down so my friends and I hiked out onto the rocks to seek further amusement. To our delight we discovered a keyhole-shaped niche in the rocks that had a sandy bottom and a fairly long channel to the sea that allowed waves to rush in and fill the round part of the keyhole with knee deep frothing water. Almost immediately the water would retreat, exposing the flat, sandy bottom. In no time we were taking death-defying, or at least wet-defying, leaps down onto the sand and scrabbling back out before the next wave would fill the basin again. To make it more of a challenge, someone had the bright idea of jumping down and writing their name in the sand before they were swamped by the incoming cold seawater.

On my turn, I had jumped down and written my name, but on the way out I dropped my hat into a puddle at the side of the keyhole floor. I loved that hat and had no intention of sending it to China.

A hat is a special bit of apparel which can serve various purposes; you can show respect by tipping or removing your hat; a hat can protect your head from the sun and rain; a hat can also be a fashion statement. You can even "keep something under your hat". Some hats are worn by members of a certain profession. Mine qualified for all of the above. It was one of those striped caps favoured by railroad engineers and I cherished it.

I had little time before the next wave came in and frothed away with my hat, so down I leapt again, grabbed my wet hat, and scrambled up chased all the way by the Pacific Ocean. Luckily my friend John lent a hand to haul me up. He said it was lucky that my hat hadn't gone out to sea, maybe on its way to Japan. While I stood there with a little of the Pacific Ocean dripping down onto my face and neck I was imagining the possible travels of my hat. That's when I came up with the idea that since I had dipped my hat in the Pacific that perhaps I should dip it into the Atlantic as well. In retrospect, it wasn't much of a reason to travel across the country, but it seemed a good idea at the time.

On the Road Again

May 1st was Blast-Off Day for my wife and me. We set out from our home on Vancouver Island early that morning. Where we live on the Island the mainland is about 50 km away. We drove about an hour to the ferry terminal in Nanaimo and arrived the prescribed half hour before sailing. After our two hour crossing the Salish Sea we had a lot of Canada to cross to get to the Atlantic Ocean. A couple of hours east at the narrow end of the Fraser Valley we pulled into Hope.

After overnighting in Hope, we left the Trans-Canada and headed into the mountains. There are currently three highways to choose from and all follow river valleys. We set out on Highway 3, the Crowsnest, travelling east through Manning Provincial Park towards the town of Princeton. The highway climbs steadily out of Hope. It wasn't long before we could see some snow off in the bush along the sides of the road. The highway winds alongside rushing rivers in the mountain valleys and on the corners you might see a grey slope of gravel and rock from the shoulder of the road right down to the frothing water and exposed rocks. Sometimes the river is only 10 or 15 feet below the highway, but sometimes it is a scary long way down; doubly so in a top-heavy walrus of a campervan.

We were definitely in the mountains now, with the manicured flat fields of the Fraser Valley far behind. The thick evergreen trees form an enormous shag carpet on the hillsides. At times, we could see ahead through the steep-sided valleys, but in some of the winding parts of the road, we couldn't even see the end of the curve. At one point, the road opened through to a clear patch in a little valley and I spotted deer tiptoeing in the drifts beside a creek that we could see below the roadway.

When I looked upward from the creek I spied a GIANT MARMOT. "Look," I cried, "a GIANT MARMOT!" Immediately, Donna pulled over, stopped engines, and dropped anchor. There it was! A GIANT MARMOT, or rather a wooden statue of the mascot of Manning Provincial Park, which rises beside the highway at the park entrance like, well, a giant rodent.

Here's a little background to explain my excitement about the marmot. You see, we generally give a pet name to our vehicles, like *The Red Racer*, which was a sporty little import; *The Green Hornet*, a little green pickup whose muffler buzzed; or, to acknowledge the embarrassment of my teenage daughters who were deeply ashamed to be seen in our boxy 4-door sedan with plaid upholstery, *The Nerdmobile*. So when we bought our present camper van a few months back, we wanted a suitable name. The van is kind of an ugly brown colour, and although we did come up with a couple of unflattering names of ugly brown things, we settled on the much more flattering, "*The Marmot.*" Marmots are brown and there are some, but not many, marmots indigenous to Vancouver Island—in fact, the Vancouver Island marmot is notably considered to be one of Canada's most endangered species.

After hearing of our name for the van, a good friend gave us a little plush toy marmot to be a kind of mascot. These little guys were sold as a fundraising item in support of a program to help this endangered Vancouver Island species. Which, I am happy to say are beginning to prosper.

He is a great mascot. Now we had a name for the van but we still needed a name for our little marmot. My wife was complaining that the names I came up with were all either dreadful or smarmy. And being a little hard of hearing, I thought she said "Let's call him Smarmy."

So now you can understand why we absolutely had to stop for the photo opportunity with *Smarmy*, our marmot, and the GIANT MARMOT. I held Smarmy close to the camera so he would look really big beside the marmot statue. Then we had fun setting up a few other poses. It was an auspicious event. Little did I know the Shit Fairy saw us enjoying ourselves.

Teenager on the loose

I was almost 18 and it was my first solo trip across the country. In early summer, I mooched my first ride in the back of a green '62 Econoline van with the guys in a rock and roll band that my cousin knew. The band was off to Edmonton. I had $86 in cash, a sleeping bag, a packsack, and a bit of a hangover.

In truth, the hangover was almost gone by the time we left New Westminster, but getting the hangover was how I hooked up with the band. I had spent most of the day before wearing dark sunglasses, drinking cola, and making few sudden moves. That was because the night before, my cousin Bob and I had fallen victim to the siren seductions of a beverage known as Double Jack.

For those of you not from that time and place, Double Jack was a kind of apple wine that was both strong and cheap. It had a lovely urine sort of colour and a bouquet like the breath of a wino eating a toffee apple. I had recently become a Double Jack user when I was introduced to the stuff by a girl who claimed it could induce a nirvana-like state when drunk in large quantities while listening to really loud Led Zeppelin music. I didn't know much about nirvana, not the band of the '80s, but rather the eastern concept of liberation, or moksha, which refers to release from a state of suffering after an often lengthy period of committed spiritual practice. Her theory was that Double Jack was a short cut that ruled out the need for years of spiritual practice. Sounded good to me. As is the case with many teenaged boys, the combination of rock music, alcohol, and a teenage girl was irresistible. Double Jack was number one with me.

Bob's place was on the mainland and the jumping off point for my hitchhiking journey. I had called him and wangled an invitation to stay over on my way to the east coast. I took the afternoon ferry and thumbed into the city. Cousin Bob made us a spaghetti dinner and I provided the wine - a small jug of the aforementioned Double Jack. As we drank it with our meal, I could tell Bob was beginning to give in to the dark side, saying, "This stuff is really not all that bad," and, "You know, this stuff is OK," and, "I don't think it will make you go blind."

The after-dinner entertainment began when we realized we had run out of Double Jack. So there we were, laughing and racing each other downhill from his apartment to the liquor store at the bottom of the street. When you are a little drunk and two of you decide to race down a steep street, the odds are that one of you will trip and get scuffed-up on the sidewalk. Well, we beat the odds. Both of us were sporting bleeding scrapes and torn clothing as we burst into the liquor store, raucously calling for a gallon jug of the stuff. The clerk looked at us a little apprehensively, then looked around, perhaps hoping for a passing cop. Not seeing any police nearby, he shrugged and reached under the counter (seeing where they kept the stuff was somewhat telling) and pulled out a gallon jug of the golden elixir. We had the decency to get out the door before the top spun off and sailed away like a mini Frisbee into the gutter. We each took a healthy snort and headed back up the street.

Most parts of the evening that followed are a bit foggy, but I do recall that we decided to phone my brother to say hi. Trouble was, he was somewhere in Australia and neither of us knew exactly where, although the name Lightning Ridge seemed about right. So, telling the overseas operator it was a matter of life and death (Bob's hamster had, in fact, died), we ended up talking to an Aussie constable who took my name and promised to *sind Kivin aout weth thi missij*.

Satisfied with our efforts, we happily called it a night. I pretty much forgot all about the phone call. I suppose Bob was roughly reminded when his phone bill came. My reminder came sometime later when I learned that the call elicited a few anxious telegrams from New South Wales starting with: INFORMED OF RALPH'S DEATH STOP PLEASE SEND DETAILS STOP, which may have created a few anxious moments for my dear old mum, too. Perhaps it was just as well I was a few thousand miles away, somewhere back east, until long after the smoke had cleared.

During our hung-over recuperation next morning, my cousin told me he knew the members of a band who were headed to Edmonton. He made a call that Sunday afternoon and found they had room for me. Early Monday morning, Bob and I stopped off on the way to his work and, after quick introductions, I grabbed my pack from the back of his pickup and threw it in the back of the van. I was on my way.

A couple hours later, we were in Hope. Like most drivers, we stopped for gas, coffee, donuts, cigarettes, and a piss. From Hope, we headed north and east on

Highway 1, the Trans-Canada through the Fraser Canyon, then at Kamloops we turned north onto the Yellowhead, which took us to Edmonton. (The shorter, modern route up the Coquihalla Canyon had not been built in those days.) The weather was grand and I hadn't a care in the world as we motored and smoked and talked and listened to music and snoozed (except the driver) from time to time. The highway was good, the mountains were impressive, and it felt like we had the world by the tail. We stopped occasionally for gas and snacks and bathroom breaks as the fuel gauge and our bladders commanded, and rolled into Edmonton on a warm Alberta spring evening.

It turned out that the house where the band members were staying was a big old place and I was invited to stay as well. Our generous hosts put together an impromptu street party and I was convinced that Edmonton was a very warm and welcoming place. We were still up at daylight, engaged in one of those momentous discussions that included both the meaning of life and which kind of peanut butter was best, but feeling talked out, and seeing no unattached female still up, I decided that as long as I was awake anyhow I might as well hit the road. After thanking my hosts, I grabbed my pack and headed for the highway. Murder was the furthest thing from my mind.

As the first car pulled over I thought I was pretty lucky to catch a ride so early in the morning and congratulated myself on my good fortune. The driver asked through the open passenger window where I was headed. When I replied I was going as far east as I could get, he seemed agreeable and then asked if I could drive. When I said yes, he looked pleased and told me to hop in because we were going to Toronto. I couldn't believe my luck as I tossed my pack into the back seat and told him my first name and stuck out my hand. He told me his name was Tom, we shook hands, and off we went.

Now I had been up all night and by the looks of the driver so had he, so we were both a little spaced out. He told me that the plan was to drive straight through to T.O. and take turns driving and sleeping, which sounded like a pretty good plan, especially the sleeping part. I was fairly chipper thinking this would turn out to be a quick trip across the prairies and through Ontario. We chatted for an hour or so about the trip as we headed towards Red Deer, but with the police and all, the ride turned out to be a lot shorter than I figured on. But I'd better keep you posted, gentle reader, with reports on our current trip and get back to the murder story later.

The Shit Fairy

We left the Giant Marmot feeling all was well. We were happy with our picture-taking and oblivious to the possibility that the Shit Fairy would strike.

For those of you unfamiliar with her, she delights in bringing small misfortunes to innocent folk. In the universe, there are forces of good and forces of evil, and she is one of the evil ones. However, she is not responsible for great evil, like wars or famines; rather, she is content to bring small miseries like a flat tire or a leak in the water heater, or when your computer hard drive gives up.

This is how the Shit Fairy struck:

The Crowsnest Highway follows quite a steep and winding path from Hope up into the Cascade Mountains. The name "Nine Mile Hill" gives you an idea of the kind of road it is. So getting back into traffic on the Crowsnest after visiting the Giant Marmot turnout requires a burst of speed and some sharp turning. We were chilled after taking pictures in the snow, so before leaving the rest area we warmed up in the van with the heater on full for a few minutes and enjoyed some hot tea poured from our thermos bottle into nice big mugs. There is a little shelf with cup-holders built into the doghouse over the engine and that's where the half-filled tea mugs rested when we set off. Unnoticed, the cell phone was perched on a ledge strategically situated above the doghouse. So when I hit the gas pedal and sped into the curve to get back on the highway, the cell phone did a pinpoint perfect dive into one of the teacups. Darn!

Yup, definitely the work of the Shit Fairy.

Note to travellers: cell phones seldom function properly after immersion in tea.

Secondary note to travellers: It spoils the tea as well.

We weren't too happy about her little prank, but we cheered up soon, when we stopped in at the Manning Park Lodge gift shop. To our delight, they had their own kind of plush marmots for sale and Smarmy fell in love with one. Although we don't want to cast aspersions on her character, she was labelled a "HOARY MARMOT" so we called her Charlotte, as in the old song:

Charlotte the harlot,

The girl I adore,

The queen of the prairie,

The cowpuncher's whore.

With Charlotte on board, we drove on towards Princeton. It was a pleasant spring day and we picnicked for lunch by the Similkameen River. Our next stop was Hedley.

Gold and Mining

Tucked beneath the impressive cliffs of Stemwinder Mountain to the west and Nickel Plate Mountain to the east, lies the charming little village of Hedley, British Columbia. The natives once called this place "Sna-za-ist" – the Striped Rock Place – on account of the coloured and striped cliffs on both sides of the canyon.

After the discovery of gold in 1897, Hedley became one of the great names in Canadian gold mining history. Named after Robert R. Hedley, manager of the Hall Smelter in Nelson, who had grubstaked many of the early prospectors, Hedley grew quickly. By 1900, it boasted a population of over 1,000 with five hotels and a large stamp mill.

The V.V. & E. railroad arrived in Hedley in 1909 to help haul the gold away at the incredible rate of more than 50,000 ounces per year. In 1936, the Mascot Mine started operation, increasing the total production to more than 1.5 million ounces of gold and in excess of 4 million pounds of copper. By that time, Hedley boasted all of the major conveniences of a small city, including a nine-hole golf course.

Between 1956 and 1957, there were several disastrous fires in the community and this, coupled with dwindling ore production from the mines, led to

Hedley's steady decline. Nowadays, Hedley is a quiet community with an approximate population of 350.

The gold, which would be worth more than $2 billion at today's prices, is long gone, and the wealth it created ended up somewhere else, as evidenced by the modest little town and the mining ruins that we could see. The little museum appears to struggle to find enough money to keep its story of the town alive. From the stairs of the museum you can see the remains of the mills that processed the ore, but they are closed to visitors for safety reasons. It's a bit of a melancholy scene, all in all.

I am including a glossary of mining terms that may help the reader better understand Hedley's history:

AMALGAMATION A process by which gold and silver are extracted from an ore by dissolving them in mercury.

CONCENTRATE A product containing the valuable metal and from which most of the waste material in the ore has been removed.

GRUBSTAKE: Finances or supplies of food, etc., furnished to a prospector on the promise of some share in any discoveries he might make.

MILL: (a) A plant in which ore is treated for the recovery of valuable metals; (b) A machine consisting of a revolving drum for the fine grinding of ores as a preparation for treatment.

SALOON: A building in which miners and their gold are separated by flushing with alcohol.

PYRITE: A hard, heavy, shiny, yellow mineral, being a sulphide of iron. It is sometimes called "fools gold."

CITIZENS: The original owners of the minerals that are removed by mining, sometimes called "fools" (see Politicians below).

POLITICIANS: Persons financed by mining companies on the promise of making laws favouring the easy extraction of minerals. Politicians promise prosperity to the citizens, who then give their mining rights to the Robber Barons.

ROBBER BARON: A businessman or banker who uses questionable practices to become powerful or wealthy (see Politicians).

ZERO: The number of times the promised prosperity of mining comes to the citizens from whom it was extracted (see Hedley).

After our morning visit to the museum, we left a donation, climbed aboard the Marmot van, and, like the Robber Barons of the past, left Hedley to its fate. We continued south on Highway 3 and stopped for a coffee break and to stretch our legs at Stemwinder Provincial Park on the banks of the Similkameen. We were the only visitors, probably because the weather was cool this early in the season. In summer, I am told, it is filled with people enjoying the river and the scenery. Although it was not too warm it was still a great stop. We tramped down to the river and explored a bit and then had a picnic lunch with the place to ourselves.

We motored along Highway 3 until Keremeos where we took a shortcut northeast on Highway3A. From there, we passed through the town of Olalla and enjoyed the farms and scenery of the mountain valleys to Penticton. We stopped for lunch and found a shop where we bought a new cell phone because of our visit from the Shit Fairy. Then it was north to Kelowna and a pleasant overnight visit with cousins we had not seen for a while. We set out after breakfast the next morning, driving up the Okanagan Valley on our way to Vernon.

A Drunk in the Night

In Vernon, we stopped at Polson Park in town to eat our lunch. We found a spot near Vernon Creek, which flows through the grounds and is bordered by lawns and flowerbeds. The park boasts a lovely Japanese garden and is well worth a visit. During lunch, I was reminiscing about the time back in 1970 when I had spent a night in the park. I was traveling west with a pretty red-haired girl that I had met in the Rockies. It was in that park near that creek when we had a run in with an obnoxious drunk. (Remember my mother's warnings?)

It was like this: I have always been a bit of a light sleeper and sat up in my sleeping bag when I heard somebody approaching. It was either very late or very early, depending on your point of view, but there was a bit of light in the sky as a rough-looking old drunk with a beer carton under his arm and less than a full set of teeth, wandered up and slurred, "Hey buddy, can I bum a shmoke?"

I was a little scared and didn't know exactly what to do. Drunks often take offence at the least thing and I didn't want to provoke him. Here I was with a girl that I didn't want to introduce to this seedy guy. I hoped the offer of my tobacco and papers would be the quickest way to get rid of him, so I dug the tobacco pouch out of my coat and passed it over. He rolled a smoke, lit it, and offered me a beer. So as not to give offence, I accepted. He asked if my buddy wanted a beer and I had to think fast.

I whispered that my buddy (who had pulled her head down into her sleeping bag with just some red hair showing) was a wild and crazy Irish guy who was a real mean son of a bitch if you woke him up. If he woke up, somebody was likely to get a punch in the face. As the drunk's brain slowly pieced together what the likely result of his uninvited visit might be, he glanced nervously at my buddy. Pressing my advantage, I suggested in a whisper that he roll a couple smokes to take with him. He rolled the smokes nervously, keeping one eye on my buddy, returned my tobacco, and promptly left.

After a minute of quiet, my buddy peeked out and said she had been kind of worried about the drunk. I tried to act as if I wasn't the least bit concerned, but I may not have fooled her. For her part, she was gracious enough to commend my quick thinking and adept mastery of our seedy visitor. She made me feel quite clever and I was very pleased thinking I had impressed her. I still smile when I think of that red-haired girl in Vernon…

Old Coots in the Kootenays

Okay, back on the present-day road. After lunch, we fired up the Marmot van and left town via Highway 6 to do a bit of exploring. The highway east from Vernon to Nakusp proved to be not good. The pavement was rough, the way was winding and hilly, and it was cold. It took much longer than we had planned as we were travelling quite slowly a lot of the time because of the bad road. Added to that, grades in the Monashee Pass area were fairly steep. We felt a little apprehensive because we met so few travellers on this empty stretch of road. If you ran into trouble out here, it might be quite a wait before someone came along.

Happily, nothing untoward happened along that lonely route. We crossed Upper Arrow Lake via the five-minute free ferry at Fauqier, and then motored north on the eastern shore along a pretty good road. A little later than had planned, we rolled into Nakusp.

At Nakusp, we headed to the hot springs, which were northeast out of town fourteen klicks on another very winding and hilly road. I suppose it's not unheard of for roads in the mountains to be hilly and winding. It might make for a delightful ride on a motorcycle gearing down and leaning into turns and twisting the throttle up into the straights, but wrestling and flogging our lumbering camper van took the shine off that apple pretty quickly. It was the difference between galloping on a horse and driving a team of unruly oxen.

There was still snow on the picnic tables when we got to the hot springs resort, but the campground was open. We signed in, found our spot, and fired up the furnace. The snow had made a little hillock about eight inches deep on the centre of our picnic table, which was in the shade, but the sun had mostly melted the snow from the gravel of our parking area. After a bit of supper and a little rest, we hiked up a steep path to the pool. There were only a few other poolers present, so we had a good quiet relax after our day of van wrangling. Warm and sleepy, we headed down the grade to the van and, thanks to the little furnace, we had a cozy night despite freezing temperatures outside.

Next morning we went for a healthy constitutional in Nakusp. The residents have made a great job of a walkway and garden overlooking Arrow Lake. You are quite high above the shore; from that vantage point it is easy to imagine the comings and goings of commercial shipping, which was a vital part of Nakusp's past. We spent an hour meandering and stopping and enjoying the views of the lake and, as we rounded a corner, we happened upon a marvellous— and unlooked-for—Japanese garden. It was a treat to just sit in such beautiful surroundings and count our blessings.

Eventually rousing ourselves, we took leave of the Nakuspidores and drove down Highway 6 through New Denver and then across the mountains via Highway 31A to Kaslo on Kootenay Lake.

We were interested to visit the historic Moyie which is a paddle steamer sternwheeler that worked on Kootenay Lake from 1898 until 1957.

After her nearly sixty years of service for the CPR, she was sold to the town of Kaslo . Today, she has been restored to her original operating condition and sits on a concrete berth at the end of Front Street. She is the world's oldest intact passenger sternwheeler. Donna and I enjoyed exploring and imagining what traveling on this sternwheeler must have been like. There is a ladies lounge at one end, a men's smoking lounge at the other, and the dining room in the middle. It was a treat to see the authenticity of the ships cook cutting food with sound effects. Also there is the video which tells about the rescue of this vessel and how it ended up being in dry dock at Kaslo. If you are interested in a little history then this is worth a visit.

Lunch at Kaslo was a picnic at the community park. Our picnic spot was not far from a daycare building and it wasn't long before we became aware that one of the kids was named Huckleberry. From the overheard remarks from the day-care we assumed that like Mark Twain's character, this Huckleberry was no stranger to mischief.

Huckleberry, you can't do that...

Huckleberry come and try this...

Huckleberry get down from there...

Huckleberry, time to go in...

Huckleberry, time to go in...

Huckleberry, time to go in.

We finished our lunch, packed up, and waved goodbye to Huckleberry, who still had not gone in. We were off south and west to Nelson for our first night of stealth camping.

Stealth Camping

Before we left home, I had been doing a little work on the Marmot van because I wasn't happy with the interior layout. I wanted to install some kind of air conditioning. In 1981, when the van was built, dashboard-controlled air conditioning had not been installed. I priced out some options and an aftermarket installation was going to be more than half of the price we paid for the van. Even if I had gathered up a system from an auto wrecker and installed what I could, I still would have been obliged to have a licensed technician complete the installation and that amount of money and effort was not what I wanted.

The solution turned out to be a home air conditioner, an inverter, and some batteries. It was not really cheap, but the price was at least reasonable to me and the install was pretty straightforward. But before I took on the job, I did a little research on van conversions. That's when I came across an article about stealth vans. Evidently these are vans that people in cities live in. The owners just move about finding unobtrusive places to park each night. With a stealth van, you don't pay rent. Cool idea!

So having been paying $30 or more a night for camping spots that weren't really even up and running, I suggested we "stealth it" and use the money to buy a meal. We agreed on the plan and it seemed a good one.

Actually, the plan was quickly modified to read: sleep in a box store parking lot. It turned out that some box stores had hatched the scheme of allowing RVs to park overnight. It actually works in the favour of the store because, instead of making a campfire, visiting with the other campers, or walking to see the river or lake or whatever, the hapless traveller sitting in the RV in the parking lot eventually succumbs to the lure of the hardware department and spends at least as much as a campsite would have cost.

So walking out of the store with our purchases, we were not particularly pleased to see that the parking lot was pretty much empty except for a couple frantic shoppers who ran in and ran out with a carton of cigarettes or a jug of milk and a couple of shady characters sitting in an old pimped-out Oldsmobile. It appeared they had a number of acquaintances who stopped in for a quick chat and perhaps were loaning our guys some money or perhaps were buying homemade jewellery. It eventually occurred to us that their transactions might have been of the unlawful kind. Seems a lot of money was changing hands and they were doing a pretty brisk trade. We decided it was not the place to be in the middle of the night. Okay. Plan B.

Plan B: Find a nice quiet residential street and park overnight. Seems simple enough. A little hitch was that we should have amended the plan to read "nice quiet *level street*." We both agreed that having your feet way up or way down was not conducive to a good night's sleep, nor was a sideways slant with everyone rolling to one side. Rolling was okay for the one who rolls toward the wall, but not for the one who either rolls out onto the floor or has to imitate a Star Trek character and become a Klingon. Unfortunately, the amended Plan B was just not well suited to the city of Nelson, which, we discovered after a thorough search, has no level streets at all. After half an hour of leaning this way and that, and rolling off the bunks, we formulated Plan C.

Plan C: In a flash of insight, I remembered a park from the tourist brochure I had perused earlier that day.

Lakeside Park lies at the edge of the West Arm of Kootenay Lake at the foot of the famous 'Orange Bridge.' Streetcar #23's tracks lead through Lakeside Park to another loop at the East entrance of the Park.

Perfect! At Lakeside Park we found a level place and even washrooms at the streetcar station. In fact, we had eaten our supper at the other end of the park earlier in the evening so it was somewhat familiar. The parking area had been pretty well populated at supper time, but now it was pretty much empty. Great! We congratulated ourselves, closed up all the curtains, and bunked down. YES! Stealth Camping could work! And it did…until about midnight.

It turns out that on Friday night about midnight on a spring evening, the youth of Nelson frequent Lakeside Park. But not as you might suppose: to stroll quietly in the moonlight by the lake and whisper the intimacies of starstruck lovers. No, the youth of Nelson are given to running and shrieking and hollering and playing hide-and-seek. During their antics, they hide behind things like, well, our Stealth Van. And then they loudly carry on an argument with someone at least a hundred yards away:

"YOU'RE BEHIND THE CAMPER VAN!"

"NO I'M NOT!"

"I CAN SEE YOU THERE!"

"NO YOU CAN'T!"

But even teenagers eventually tire and move on, and after an hour or two of fun, all was quiet again and we got back to sleep.

Now I suppose we could be forgiven for not taking into account that some of the tracks near the park were not for Streetcar #23. Being used to our quiet little Vancouver Island E & N Railway "Dayliner" train, which had one car and used to run north through our neighbourhood one way to tell us to stop for lunch at 12:00 noon, and back south again at 2:30 to announce afternoon coffee time, we may be allowed to use that as an excuse for being naive about rail traffic. We actually liked to see our cute little train, with its two or three passengers, toot on by as it made its way up and down the Island.

So when the first hideous roaring and clanking of an enormous, berserker freight train not 20 feet away rattled us out of our sleep and nearly out of our bunks, we assumed that it must be a solitary, frantic train with its unfortunate crew hurrying home to loved ones after some unavoidable delay in their daylight journey. The poor guys; getting home so late. After about the fifth train, we realized that these bloody trains run all night and that some evil genius had contrived to route all the rail traffic in North America through Nelson between 1:00 and 5:00 am. As is often the case with those who choose to share life's joys and calamities, some of us were not ready to jointly accept blame for a bad plan. There were even suggestions made that I, personally, should accept responsibility for "THIS STUPID STEALTH VAN IDEA." Fortunately, the shaking of the van and the hideous squealing and banging of the steel wheels of the passing trains drowned out further discussion of culpability.

Like Voltaire's cheerful Candide, whose motto was *Everything turns out for the best in this best of all possible worlds*, I optimistically pointed out the happy news that we were certainly up early enough to be sure to get a space on the first ferry from Balfour to Crawford Bay, which we did. Yes, we certainly arrived early enough, but some of us were not particularly bright and cheerful at the Crawford Bay landing.

However, our spirits rose when, amazingly enough to us Islanders, who are charged exorbitant fares for ferry travel, we read that… "The inland ferries operate under private contract with the Ministry of Transportation and Infrastructure." ALL INLAND FERRIES ARE FREE OF CHARGE TO USERS. Free Ferry? What a wonderful idea.

Thirty-five minutes later, we were across the lake. About five minutes after we disembarked at the eastern ferry landing, we stopped at a storybook log building along Highway 3A. It sits at the edge of a clearing with a big welcoming circular drive and parking area. Facing the road is a diamond-shaped window in the gable with a pair of brooms making a V shape beneath it. The sign below says, "North Woven Broom Company" and sure enough, they make brooms. It was early and still quite cool, so the doors were shut, but we were welcomed in when we knocked and were ushered to a cozy place with a woodstove that had the place nice and warm. Wow! They had a lot of brooms! We nosed around and chatted with the owner and a girl who worked for her. We learned that they are a family-run cottage industry, making brooms in summer and heading south to gather materials in the winter. There were brooms of every size and description, but the

Marmot van didn't have a whole lot of room for a big broom, so we came away with a couple of delightful tiny ones.

Across the road from the broom company there was the Kootenay Forge Blacksmith Shop, which caught my interest, and we spent some time there as well. We didn't buy any metalwork but we enjoyed talking to the owner and poking around. They had some beautiful ironwork pieces on display and some copper and glasswork as well.

The road down the east side of Kootenay Lake was rough and winding. Rough because it was the end of winter and the potholes hadn't been repaired yet, and winding because it follows the contours of the lake. It might have been more pleasant but for the manic logging truck drivers. They constantly tailgated us and we pulled over as often as we could to get rid of them. We were glad to get to Creston.

The approach to Creston was marvellous and the valley was a wonderful surprise. Springtime number 3. Springtime number 1 was before we left home. After the daffodils and tulips were finished, we had loaded up the Marmot van and set out. Outside of Hope we were back into snow until we arrived in the Okanagan, where spring number 2 was in full bloom. It was back to winter in the mountains and then "ta-dah!" cherry blossoms in Creston: Springtime number 3.

The valley is like a secret hideout in the mountains. As I often do, I began to imagine finding a nice place and moving there. I could see myself with a little cabin overlooking the valley, or maybe a little farm with an orchard. So wanting to do a little exploring, we went to the info centre.

Free Samples

This was our third info centre. At the first, in Hope, we checked in for maps and brochures. The second was a stop at Nakusp, where we got our first hint about some peculiarities of info centres. But here in Creston, the true nature of info centres was beginning to emerge.

The name "info centre" might describe the racks of brochures and maps reasonably accurately, but if you are hoping for a person who is intimately familiar with the area and its attractions, you are likely in for a letdown. In the Creston info centre, the two young women on duty looked very much like what they turned out to be: university students on summer jobs. Bright, cheerful, and willing to help. The one who was across the counter from us admitted that she was not all that familiar with the area because she had just moved to Creston for this summer job. BUT, she did know that there was a beer brewery and that there were tours and **free samples**.

We were the only people in the place. At the mention of the brewery, the other young woman came to join the discussion, adding that the brewery tour was great and there were **free samples**. Under interrogation, however, the other woman admitted that she, too, had moved here for the summer job and really hadn't had much of a chance to get to know the area. Come to think of it, in Nakusp, the woman in the info centre was also a new arrival in the town. Hmmmm....

We had our lunch in the community park and decided to take the advice of the infocentre women and went to tour the brewery. It turned out well.

They have a Sasquatch statue in front of the brewery, so we had some fun with a photo-op with Smarmy, our mascot, and *"Sas"* the Sasquatch. Once inside, we found we had missed the scheduled tour of the brewing operation, but we did enjoy a **free sample,** and much to the delight of Smarmy, we found a little stuffed *"Sas the Sasquatch"* in the souvenir section, who joined our growing family of stuffed animals.

We only had a few samples so it was safe to drive on towards Cranbrook during the afternoon and regrettably passed on a visit to Yahk, where we later learned you can purchase a T-shirt with the boast, <u>I've been to Yahk and Back</u> printed on it.

The info centre in Cranbrook was *"closed for the season."* What season? Hockey season? Hunting season? Monsoon season? Mating season? Who knows? Just one more aspect of the weird and wonderful world of info centres.

We spied the train museum which was advertised in a guidebook we had with us and had an interesting visit complete with a tour of old rail cars from years gone by. Smarmy was making a fool of himself for the camera as usual, pretending to be an historical figure travelling by train. He even got me to try sitting on the seats and lying on the beds when nobody was looking.

We had planned to spend the night at an RV park near Fernie, which we had picked out from the camping guidebook, but as we drove up we didn't fancy the place. It looked a lot like a residential trailer park with a few temporary spots to park at one end. It was a little too exposed for us. So we motored on.

As it turned out, that was an excellent decision. We made our way to Sparwood and stayed at Mountain Shadows Campground, one of the nicest of our whole trip. There is a woodsy-looking log building housing the office and forested sites all around. We arrived when the attendant was running an errand, so we picked out a nice spot and settled in. After supper we went to the office and signed in, paid the reasonable fee, and even found out we could use our laptop with a wireless feed. I caught up with my emails and Donna used the showers, reporting that they were great. I followed suit and very contentedly, we called it a night. We woke up to a dump of snow and were pleased that the Marmot van's furnace was working well. It was May 8th.

After breakfast, we thanked our host and got a few tips on finding supplies in Sparwood. We got what we wanted at a few of the shops in town and took a photo of the world's largest dump truck. I decided not to make any jokes about the world's largest dump truck. The nature of those trucks and the job they do became clear when we looked up at the surrounding mountains and saw that the entire top of one of them had been cut off. The sides of the mountain just stopped and the top was gone. Just like the coal miners in John Prine's song *Paradise* where the mountain was hauled away.

On to Alberta

We made our way along Highway 3 following the crow signs towards Crowsnest Pass. The highway was a pleasant drive along a river valley with lots to see. We counted three mountain sheep and four elk. At Summit Lake, we pulled over at a stop of interest sign to learn that we were in a pass through the Rocky Mountains and it was downhill to both the Pacific and the Atlantic oceans. It was a great day to be on the top of the continent.

Surprisingly, we were stopped at a police checkpoint, which was advertised as a vehicle safety check. Evidently our vehicle was not the kind the police were looking for, because we were directed to an express lane and, after a cursory look in the driver's window, our vehicle was declared safe to drive on into Alberta. I was relieved because I suspected we had a broken spring courtesy of the amazing potholes in the Kootenays, and I knew one of our backup light bulbs was burned out.

Learning a little history of the region, we found that police checks had been common for a very long time. The Municipality of Crowsnest Pass still celebrates Rum Runner Days in recognition of their part in running booze to quench the thirst of Albertans. Drinking alcohol in "Wild Rose Country" was illegal, according to temperance laws in effect from 1916 to 1923. Eventually, alcohol prohibition was given up because it was agreed that the policy was too hard to police. Perhaps the current checkpoint had something to do with trade in tobacco, or maybe cannabis, both of which seem equally as hard to police and at least as commonplace as alcohol.

We kept heading east on Highway 3 until the junction with Highway 2, where we turned north. After a bit, we went west on Highway 785 to find Head-Smashed-In Buffalo Jump. It was well marked, on a good road, and well worth the time to visit. The interpretive centre at Head-Smashed-In blends into the ancient sandstone cliff. It conceals an amazing interior. There are five levels inside with exhibits depicting the ecology, mythology, lifestyle, and technology of Blackfoot peoples, and interesting and easy to understand information explaining the archaeological evidence.

We spent time visiting each of the exhibits as we moved up the levels inside, eventually making our way to the top, where we went out into a cool and windy day and looked over the actual jump. It was impressive to see the use of the terrain and the deadly drop. We marvelled at the bravery and cunning that it must have taken to kill those big hairy buffaloes.

The highlight of our visit was when we came inside again to warm up and managed to strike up a conversation with one of the local men who worked at the centre. He explained how the buffalo would come to feed above the jump when the grass dried off on the surrounding plains. Then an extremely brave hunter would cover himself with a buffalo skin and mimic a calling baby buffalo to lure the herd closer and closer to the cliffs. Then, suddenly, the rest of the people would come out of hiding and panic the beasts over the cliff.

I don't think I'd want to be the one to be the baby buffalo. You'd be between the buffaloes and the edge of the cliff and you might want to get out of the way in a hurry!

Then there were the marmots! Up to the adoption of Smarmy as our mascot, I'd really had very little experience with marmots and even less knowledge about them. Now marmots were turning up everywhere, including here at the buffalo jump. The little rascals were darting in and out of fissures and holes all over the place. Who knew there were Buffalo Marmots?

We went on to High River and spent the night there. It was like a lot of other prairie towns at the end of winter. There was still some dirty snow here and there with little trickles of meltwater finding their way through the accumulated sand and dirt left by the road crews all winter. The winter's rubbish was either flattened onto the road surface or blowing around with the dust that the wind toyed with. There were no real signs of green growth anywhere to interrupt the grey-brown grass and trees. No wonder spring is such a delight on the prairies.

I don't like city driving. Calgary, being the largest city in the country geographically, requires more city driving to pass through it than any other city in Canada. It was a rat race. Lots of traffic and high-speed highway driving. We cheered when we saw the "You are leaving Calgary sign."

The highway north to Edmonton was flat and straight and we soon left all traces of the mountains behind. The pavement was different. All cross the prairies the highways were…clunky. There were black lines like joints across the paving and as we drove they set up a continuous clunk, clunk,clunk, as the tires bumped over each one. I was to learn that this clunkety-clunk paving was pretty common.

We powered through to Edmonton and were relieved to stay with family for a few days. It also gave us a chance to get the broken rear spring repaired on the van. We were amazed at the growth of the city. Houses were popping up like mushrooms. We visited a newly built neighbourhood, which had been fields the year before. There were streets and streets of brand new houses for sale. It was a shock to our rural systems.

We said our thank-yous and good-byes and headed east on Highway 16, the Yellowhead. It is also a Trans-Canada route. We speculated that the Yellowhead image on the road signs could be a bird or even another kind of marmot until we realized it was a "yellow head".

When I had been hitchhiking so many years earlier, I had gone south from Edmonton and stayed on the other Trans- Canada, which is the southern route, so I should finish that part of the story before we follow the Yellowhead route.

Murder?

To recap: I thought I was pretty lucky to catch a ride out of Edmonton so early in the morning and congratulated myself on my good fortune. The driver asked through the open window where I was headed. When I replied I was going as far east as I could get, he seemed agreeable and asked if I could drive. When I said yes, he looked pleased and told me to hop in because we were going to Toronto. I couldn't believe my luck. I tossed my pack into the back seat and told him my first name and stuck out my hand. He said his name was Tom, we shook hands, and off we went.

I had been up all night; by the looks of the driver so had he, so we were both a little spaced-out. As he told me that the plan was to drive straight through to T.O. and take turns driving and sleeping. I was pretty chipper thinking this would turn out to be a quick trip across the prairies to Ontario, but with the murder and all it turned out to be a lot shorter ride than I figured on.

We chatted for an hour or so about the trip as we headed towards Red Deer. But because we were both tired we each drifted into our own thoughts and we were quiet for a while. Tom said nothing as we drove into Red Deer. I thought he was looking for a gas station while we drove around a bit. I was puzzled when we pulled into the police station. Tom was a little vague when he told me he had to check on something. So I sat in the car and rolled a smoke, lit it, and started to calculate the drive to Toronto. I pulled out my map and guessed somewhere around two or three days if we went straight through. I had finished my smoke and I was still looking down studying my highway map when a loud, serious, male voice came through the open window and asked me, "Please get out of the car, Sir."

I looked up and saw two of Her Majesty's finest and I got out of the car. They really were serious about something and they asked if I had any belongings in the car. I told them my pack was in the back seat and was just going to reach in and get it when I realized that suddenly my arms were held quite tightly and I was advised to stand still, please, which I did. I asked what the matter was and was told that the officers wanted to ask me a few questions. So one policeman collected my pack and we all went into the police station. I asked after Tom and was told he was unavailable.

They took me into a room with only a table and a couple of chairs and offered me a cup of coffee. I sat down and one put my pack on the end of the table and began to go through it. The other one asked me how I knew Tom. I explained that I was headed to the east coast and had just hitched a ride, which, when you think about it, wasn't a very good alibi. Evidently, the guy rummaging through my pack didn't find much of interest and even grimaced a bit when he came to my socks and underwear.

They were quite thorough and asked several questions over again as they went along. They wanted to know what Tom had spoken about. Had he mentioned anything about the previous evening? Had

Tom talked about a fight or disagreement? Was I aware that there was a rifle in the trunk?

After interrogating me, they went out and left me alone for a while. Then one of them came in and told me Tom had turned himself in because he had an argument and shot someone the night before in some town north of Edmonton.

I had certainly landed in a sticky situation. He told me that they believed I was simply in the wrong place at the wrong time. I agreed vigorously. I was told to collect my things and then I was given a ride to the edge of town. I never heard anything more about Tom or the Red Deer RCMP. I didn't mind.

Ukrainians

Meanwhile, back in the present, heading east on the Yellowhead, we set our sights on the Ukrainian Cultural Heritage Village, where, as advertised:

There's something for everyone, located 25 minutes or 50 km (30 miles) east of Edmonton on Highway 16, just 3 km (1.8 miles) east of Elk Island National Park.

We took a picture of Smarmy at the entrance to the village, but it didn't really look open for business. When we had parked and walked to the main building, we were told that the season opening of the museum was a couple of days away. We were as heartbroken as the Griswolds when Wallyworld was shut. But after explaining that this was a very important stop on our trek across the country, and that we were not likely to come back this way, and that Donna's grandparents had been pioneers in the area, a very kind woman gave us dispensation to wander around the facility.

It was great! The reconstruction job was terrific. It was as if we had stepped back into the past and were visiting the settlers. There were both farm sites and the re-created prairie town.

Our first stop was a *bordei* (Ukrainian: *бордей*), a type of dugout-style shelter, something between a sod house and a log cabin. I was amazed by the ingenuity of the builders. Using what was at hand, they had come up with a dwelling that cost them virtually no money, would service in the harsh prairie conditions, and most importantly, would allow them fairly quickly to get on with the business of creating a farm.

The bordei was built into a bank. From the outside, the roots and grass of the stacked sods were visible. They served as covering for the A-frame roof/walls. The triangular front end of the bordei was smoothed clay or plaster with a wooden door set to the right of centre. Inside, the poles of the A-frame showed how the thing was put together. The homemade table and benches, and the plaster surrounding the stove, gave the whole thing a look of competent and ingenious settlers. I was very impressed and wistfully toyed with the idea of building one myself, but after some consideration I figured they were not suitable for the west coast. I remember my dad telling me that the prairie sod house his family had lived in was drippy and soggy in wet weather. As many know, Vancouver Island gets more than its fair share of wet weather.

We ventured further through time and space and came to a farm as it might have been several years after the time of the bordei. The buildings here were made of logs and sawn lumber and there was shelter for livestock. We were able to talk to one of the staff members who was disking a field with a team of horses. It was clear from his conversation that he knew and loved horses and was very happy to be able to keep alive this piece of farm history. I poked in a few of the buildings and was delighted to discover a small flock of chickens. What is a small farm without chickens?

From the farm, we sauntered into the town and nosed around the shops and churches. I took a few moments to daydream inside the schoolhouse; not an uncommon pastime in a schoolhouse on a sunny spring day. The rows of standard iron and wood desks, the walls covered in chalkboards, and the picture of the queen were familiar because they were similar to the ones I grew up with in the little country school I attended as a boy.

We walked back to the interpretive centre and thanked the woman who had let us tour. As we were leaving, we came upon the students who were to spend their summer "being" the inhabitants. They were very welcoming and allowed us to take a few photos with them. A few had a very steep learning curve if they were to live the life of times past. Their costumes and Ukrainian language skills were great, but when we spied a few of the young men and women trying to split firewood with an axe for the first time, I was too frightened to watch for long. I winced at every chop and could see that axe very easily doing harm to someone. We hurried off to the van before anyone lost any body parts.

Back on the highway, we knew we were now behind the "koubassa curtain" because we were fast approaching Mundare, HOME OF THE GIANT SAUSAGE! We pulled in near the corner of Sawchuk Street and Stawnichy Drive and parked the van so we could see the sights. We took Smarmy along for the photo shoot, but somehow the pics didn't turn out as well as hoped- they just did not do justice to the giant sausage. There was also a very weird technicolour blue buffalo in a glass case, which made me glad I had someone with me to confirm that it was really there!

We took a look around town and made a stop at the sausage factory, which is the pride and joy of eastern Alberta. Good sausage, I am told, is as good as legal tender. If you serve it, you will be a successful host; if you bring along some tasty sausage, you are sure to be a welcome guest. We loaded up with a few rings.

Back on the highway, visions of Vegreville's famous *pysanka* were egging us on. Turning onto Highway16A,.we easily found the Elks/Kinsmen Park, which hosts the famous *World's Largest Easter Egg*, the Visitor Information Center, and the Municipal Campground.

We spotted the egg on its knoll and parked the Marmot van. There is a paved path across the grassy field to the Giant Egg. The *World's Largest Pysanka* was built about 1974 or '75. It really is quite a sight on its pillar in the sky. The bright colors and symbols stand out cheerfully against the prairie dome, especially in the early spring when not much else is showing any colour yet. We got some photos of Smarmy and the egg and set our sights on Saskatchewan. Two or three bends in the road and we were there.

Saskatchewan: Easy to Draw
Hard to Spell

Lloydminster! The Yellowhead Highway goes right through the town on an east west axis. It is advertised as a border town. The provincial border does run north-south down the middle of 50th Ave. There isn't much of a border marker though. There are a couple of markers about as high as telephone poles but no signs other than the ones advertising hamburgers, fried chicken, steaks and gas. There is no wall, no barricade, no barbed wire, no border guard not even a customs office or even an infocentre. But I suppose though it was disappointing from an excitement point of view it was a good thing because we were smuggling in a load of Alberta koubassa.

"Adios Alberta! Hello Saskatchepewchewan!"

On to Maidstone! According to the town's webpage Maidstone is a friendly community situated in west central Saskatchewan at the junction of Highway 16 and Highway 21 North between Saskatoon and Edmonton. Maidstone is located in one of the most affluent rural municipalities in the province, rich in agriculture and oil activities. Maidstone is the land of canola and purebred cattle in the heart of *the heavy crude.*

Unfortunately, the Maidstone municipal campground was having a little trouble with their water system when we arrived. The trouble was, there was no water. We made a compromise and got a free electrical hookup for the night. The girl looking after the place lived up to the friendly community billing. To return the good wishes, Donna left her a jar of homemade jam. The residents we saw seemed completely affable; never did meet anyone you'd call *"the heavy crude."*

That cold prairie wind had got up before we did, so we didn't hang around much after breakfast. We just pointed the van southeast and drove to North Battleford. The sky was grey and the fields were about the same. The poor old Marmot van is not good in a wind or at breakneck speeds (over 80 km/h), so in addition to the cold and dreary landscape, we had to wrestle and cajole and occasionally slow right down to soothe the skitterish Marmot van through the gusts.

North Battleford was just a quick stop for us because we had our sights set on Saskatoon, which I believe roughly translates to "many cousins and aunties." So we fuelled up and whipped the Marmot back onto the windy highway and horsed our way to Saskatoon. As we passed the outdoor museum on the way out of town we made a note to stop in next time through. We were to learn that the Western Development Museum of Saskatchewan actually has four venues in four different cities.

In retrospect, we were a little too laissez-faire with our schedule throughout the trip and often popped in on folks out of the blue. But in our defence, the vagaries of travel often trump the best schedules, so to avoid having people we promised to visit unhappily waiting for us, we chose to touch bases when we were getting close. Turns out, a day or so of warning is a much better idea than an hour or so, especially if the folks you wish to drop in on are working. Unfortunately for the folks in Saskatoon, we had yet to acquire this bit of traveler's wisdom. We said we would see them after work.

So we decided to tour Saskatoon for the afternoon. The highlight of our tour was our visit to the Western Development Museum. For me, this turned out to be a special treat because I enjoy things mechanical and I delight in pioneer history. The museum was everything I could have wished for.

Now I am not a young man, but I don't think I should be classified as an antique just yet. However, when I was a boy, we had a little farm and no money so we did most things by hand or with tired old machinery. So when I come across hand tools and old machinery in a museum it's a bit like bumping into old friends. My wife always indulges my reminiscing when I point out to her a hay rake, or a scythe, or a crosscut saw, or a cream separator and tell her how we used them when I was a kid. She really is quite patient with me.

As we walked along, Smarmy noticed a display about gophers. He was aghast to learn about Gopher Day. On May 1, 1917, tens of thousands of kids throughout the province were let out of classes to compete in Saskatchewan's first official Gopher Day.

Armed with poison, snares, traps, and guns, they were sent into the fields by their teachers to wage war with the "enemy of production." By sundown, the children had exterminated more than half a million of the pesky rodents. There was the special Gopher

Shield which was awarded to the school where the largest number of gopher tails were turned in.

Knowing that our parents and grandparents were very familiar with the sod houses, horse-drawn machinery, and homemade foods in the displays gives us pause to imagine their lives. This particular museum knocks the socks off any others I have seen. Not only are the displays intriguing, but the whole layout and design lets the visitor not just imagine but actually enjoy an afternoon of time travel. Promenading down the recreated street with its sights and sounds and smells is magical. Do take a look if you are in Saskatoon.

Another delight of Saskatoon is prairie hospitality. The folks there gave us a prodigal welcome. We felt like we were home and dry. Good company and good food for the next couple of days and we had a chance to relax and get out of the Marmot van. It was a delight to catch up with family and have a few tours around the city. It never seems to me that I am getting older on the inside and I am sure that is the same for most people, but when I see the changes of age on others' faces, I am always shocked by the passing of time and have to admit that I am not immune. The years slip away faster and faster as I get older and the little ones grow up in a flash. We enjoyed meeting the little ones and catching up with the other oldsters.

But, onward and upward, or rather eastward. So we headed out towards Yorkton. Our next stop turned out to be Veregin, which is designated as a national historic site. The spelling of the name of the town, Veregin, does not match the spelling of the name of the man, Peter Verigin. As my wife has discovered with her genealogy research this a very common an often frustrating error which reflects the misspelling of unfamiliar names. In this case the CPR misspelled the name.

Wikipedia states:

The headquarters of the organization of Community Doukhobors, Peter Verigin's Christian Community of Universal Brotherhood (CCUB), was located in Veregin since the organization's incorporation in 1917 until its move to Brilliant [near Castlegar], British Columbia.

Even though the majority of the Doukhobors moved from Saskatchewan to British Columbia even earlier, the Saskatchewan years loom large in their history. This is why Veregin was chosen by Doukhobor organizations as the site to celebrate the 60th, 75th, and 100th anniversaries of their arrival to Canada in 1899.

We stopped in because a friend had told us that a relative of his had lived there and we were curious. The buildings were closed up when we wandered around the grounds. There was a big, two storey house facing an open space with buildings around the sides. It was a little cool and windy, so we were making a quick tour when I noticed smoke coming out of one of the outbuildings. We found an open door and when we halloed, we were met by a couple who invited us in.

They were baking bread, a lot of bread – loaves and loaves and loaves of it. They were preparing for a big group coming to visit on the weekend. The ovens were huge and had wood fires built inside. I had never seen that before and was given a complete explanation of heating the ovens by building wood fires inside them while the bread rose and then cleaning out the fire and ash and baking in those heated up ovens. They could bake 22 loaves at once. By the look of things, it was simple and foolproof. I am sure, though , that like so many skills it appears easy and trouble-free to the casual observer. I am certain that the good results are the result of experience and expertise. We thanked our guides for their time and continued eastward.

Next stop was Canora to visit more cousins on a grain farm. Once more we were warmly welcomed and fussed over, which made us feel pretty special. We got a chance to catch up on things over a hearty meal and enjoy an evening filling up on information and anecdotes about life on a grain farm. I had no idea that the whole business was such a gamble. Not only the growing, which is a parade of possible disasters, but selling the grain is another real gamble. If they can get the grain harvested and stored safely in fall, the farmers can get a higher price in spring. But there is the added stress of knowing that if the grain sits too long into spring, it may spoil.

Each morning, the farmers get a market report, which zeroes in on different prices and trends. They check prices throughout the day and keep in touch from the fields. Like gamblers at a card table, they have to decide the point at which they play their cards. And I thought you just planted the seeds and waited.

Everyone was up early to help get set up for seeding. I tagged along and helped load up some seed and fertilizer. I had to be pretty careful emptying the sacks because some canola seed sells for $700 for a fifty pound sack. With a huge train of machinery hooked on behind the tractor, it's possible to cultivate, seed, and fertilize in one pass. As we watched our host head down the drive on his tractor, the parade of equipment he towed was akin to an agricultural travelling circus.

Glimpsing life on a working grain farm in spring made us realize what luxury it was for us to have the time to holiday across the country. We visited one more auntie in Yorkton for lunch and then headed east to Manitoba.

Homophobia Part 1

I took the southern route across Saskatchewan back in 1970. It was there that I got tangled up with more guys my mother might have worried about. Of course, when that light blue '67 Valiant pulled over to pick me up outside Medicine Hat, Alberta, that morning, I had no idea what I was getting into. The two guys in the front looked well groomed, not like the long-haired guys I'd travelled to Edmonton with. I tossed my pack into the back seat, glad to be anywhere but standing on the highway looking out on a sea of grass.

When they told me they had been on vacation in Vancouver and that they were headed back to London, Ontario, I congratulated myself on my good fortune. As that Valiant chased after the ever-elusive prairie horizon, I learned that they had found Vancouver to be a marvellous place and that they were seriously considering looking for jobs (in banking or accounting, or whatever they did) and relocating to the west coast. I was pleased to contribute that I had, in fact, been born and lived some of my early years in Vancouver and that I had lots of cousins and a couple of married siblings there. (It's always contingent upon hitchhikers to be agreeable and to offer what they can in the way of conversation in lieu of contributing any money to the expedition.)

So we chatted on during the day as we motored across Saskatchewan and into Manitoba. However, from our conversation, I began to get the feeling that these guys were more like an old married couple than a couple of young bucks out on a tear. As they talked about their new friends in Vancouver and their old friends in London, I realized that their mannerisms and topics didn't resemble the male conversations with loggers and college students that I was used to. They didn't talk about women or beer. I eased back into my seat and tried to puzzle these guys out.

I guess they noticed my unease and Larry, the passenger, asked me what was up. I replied that nothing was amiss, but he then began to nod to his partner and nonchalantly asked if I hadn't realized that they were *queers*.

Queers? I was completely taken off guard. I didn't have much background to work with. It took me a minute. My brain whirled trying to come up with some understanding. Queers? Queers? Oh!Oh! Homos!

Remember, this was 1970, and being 17 and from the sticks, this was totally unfamiliar ground and more than a little worrisome. All I had to go on was coarse jokes about lonely loggers and vague but scary admonitions about what was likely to happen to young guys in prison. And now here I was in a car full of homosexuals who would probably do terrible things to me and then murder me and leave my abused body in a rest area! My brain was sounding claxons and sirens. I was doomed!

I realized Larry was looking at me. I had the sinking feeling he was reading my mind. I suppose I wasn't wearing the poker face I had hoped for.

Larry said, "You know, homosexuals."

I said, "No, I didn't know."

I added that I wasn't. Larry laughed and said they had already figured that out. So I lied and said I wasn't worried, but with all my heart I hoped the car engine would quit and I could bail out and make a run for it. Or a cop would pull us over for a broken tail light. Please, God. Anything! I didn't want to end up a sad story in a rural Manitoba newspaper.

Rustling?

Speaking of Manitoba, back to our current journey. On our first afternoon in Manitoba we stopped in a free campground in Russel. The town maintains it and there is no charge. As a matter of fact, it's probably worth it for the local businesses to operate this free campground. We shopped for groceries and some souvenirs and even managed to find a dust cap for our propane tank. The cap had been missing at least since Saskatoon, and I figured it was probably being held for ransom at a service station in Lloydminster. The young man at the hardware department took one look and said that the dust caps on ammonia fertilizer tanks were a good match and got us two (one for a spare) for a couple bucks. Gotta love those Russellers!

The next day we stopped in Minnedosa. It really was a pleasant discovery. There was a heritage village that we enjoyed. There is the cheerful yellow painted wooden Hunterville Presbyterian Church built in 1904, a rural school, and a 1910 period home. In this age of alternate energy sources it was interesting to see a working windmill, and working water wheel. The trappers' cabin, blacksmith shop, and old log stable also gave us a glimpse into various aspects of pioneer life.

When we climbed the lookout tower, we could see Minnedosa Lake, the beach and campground, the

Bison Park, the Heritage Village, and the Rotary Suspension Bridge. What a great place to take pictures! The bison captured our interest especially because we could see baby bison. We crept along the trails hoping to get some photos of the little ones and were happily rewarded. We whispered along the fence and peered through the brush until we found a clear spot where we got a couple of shots of the fuzzy calves goofing around. Minnedosa was a great place to take a break, but eventually we had to load up and continue our journey in the afternoon.

We drove on to Portage la Prairie. In central Portage la Prairie, there is a peninsula known as Island Park, bounded by an oxbow lake called Crescent Lake. The island is a great stop. The park boasts Portage Industrial Exhibition, which hosts various agricultural competitions, a midway, and an outdoor water park for the youngsters. For those who want to relax there is an extensive arboretum, a large pen to see deer (they like carrot sticks), a duck pond, and various monuments. For exercise visitors will find playgrounds, walking trails, tennis courts and an 18-hole golf course. We had a great visit. We toured around the "island" and had our supper in the picnic area.

It was in Portage that the stealth camping notion resurfaced, but only for a moment. The stealth camping in residential Nelson was still a bit of a sore spot with some of us so as a compromise we decided to try to camp in a box store parking lot again. There was a truck towing a trailer at rest in the parking lot, and when I knocked and asked the fellow who came to the door, he pleasantly told me that he was pretty sure we could camp there and that he did this lots and it was great. It would have been great except, guess what?

Yep, *all night trains*. It seems that the same evil trains that drove us nuts in Nelson had all managed to come east to Portage to hound us again. But the joke was on them because the trains really didn't bother us all that much. Their noise was drowned out by the roaring and booming of a raging prairie thunderstorm, a very interesting prairie weather phenomenon for meteorologists and stormwatchers, I'm sure. The lightning flashes drew our attention first to one direction and then another. It was a bit like having an elusive flash camera recording the fear and frustration on our faces. Again, in Candide fashion, I remarked that, in fact, with the pounding of the rain and a leak in the roof which began dripping on my head, it seemed as if the trains were not even there at all.

Next stop Winnipeg. There was still residual rain from the storm the night before so we didn't spend too much time outdoors. We did a drive-by photo of Portage and Main, Winnipeg's infamous street corner. Growing up I was often told that it was the coldest, windiest street corner in Canada. On this bleak, grey, rainy morning I was inclined to believe it.

We stopped at the Automobile Association info centre and were rewarded with maps and knowledgeable suggestions on what was worth seeing in the city and the area. It turns out that we were at the eastern end of the Yellowhead Highway which is also part of the Trans-Canada highway system. In the west, the highway begins at Masset, British Columbia, on Haida Gwaii continues south along Graham Island to Skidegate. It then connects via ferry to Prince Rupert. From there it crosses through the Rockies by way of the Yellowhead Pass which gives the highway its name. The Yellowhead travels through Edmonton and Saskatoon onto Winnipeg. (We were to take an additional portion of the northerly Trans-Canada route through Ontario on our way home.)

The woman who helped us was a delight. She loaded us up with road maps and brochures and we had a chance to ask how far away everything was and how much things cost. She had the answers to all our questions! We decided to tour "The Forks" and then go to Lower Fort Garry. It was a treat to actually get useful information at an info centre because, across the country, more centres than we could count were simply not open. Even the ones that were open seldom kept useful hours. The best example of uselessness was the info centre that was only open on odd Tuesday afternoons from 1:00 p.m. to 2:30 p.m..

Not that every info centre we actually found open for business was staffed with competent guides. There was the Spanish-speaking exchange student who kept us working so hard at helping her to understand our questions that we gave up on the answers. It was like a weird game of charades. And there were many info centres that were staffed by someone's niece who needed a summer job, but who wasn't from there. We acquired an ability to spot these nepotistas at a glance. As often as not, they would look up from their nail polishing or computer solitaire games or grudgingly interrupt their phone conversation and explain that they actually lived somewhere else and were only here for the summer, and the maps were $2.50. The clear winner of the award for supporting the family students was the centre with three of these nieces, none of whom had any idea about the place where they were. Although to their credit, they were cheerfully ignorant, and all three were very happy to give us no useful information.

If you go to an info centre and expect to get no real info, you are likely as not to come away with your expectations met. Please bear in mind that even with staff members who know their area, it may be the case that you may be asking a question whose answer is culturally unknown. That's what happened when I went into an info centre in Calgary and asked the fellow in the cowboy getup behind the counter where I might visit public gardens. Public gardens?? He squinted painfully and glanced toward the sky. I could almost see my poor question hopelessly lost, wandering forlornly across the vast prairie of his mind with no hope of an answer.

We parked the Marmot van at the Forks parking lot, and after a cursory visit to the plaza with its dripping canopy, we went inside and toured the market at, *"The Forks, Where the Red and Assiniboine Rivers Meet."* It was warm inside, but with all the other wet steaming visitors it felt more like a jungle, especially in the food court, with all the moisture from cooking. We had a forgettable lunch, went outside and looked around for the advertised boat tours, which were not running due to wet weather and high water. We fired up the Marmot van and headed to Lower Fort Gary, which was well worth it because we arrived in time for the Victoria Day Celebrations.

The Fort itself was an interesting stop because, not only were the structures and artifacts set up as they had been in the past, but the place was peopled with guides and workers in period costume who carried on life as it had been in the days of the fur trade. We got to listen to the speech given by the acting governor and, best of all, we got free cake!

After the cake, we wandered around and visited with a young man chiselling out a timber to repair the hinge on a door in a log building and were invited into a teepee to talk to a metis woman about life at the fort. Even though it was a cool, damp day, the inside of the teepee was cozy thanks to a little fire and an ingenious windscreen. We saw one of the wooden boats used by the fur traders, which caught my interest because I have a wooden boat at home. However, the cool weather eventually got the better of us and we set off for the van.

Rather than drive back to Winnipeg, we decided to take a secondary highway and headed east with a plan of rejoining the Trans-Canada near the Ontario border. Then, about an hour out of Selkirk, we were surprised to run out of prairie. Just like that! Rocks, rocks, and more rocks - and lakes and trees and more rocks. The Canadian Shield.

To add to the feeling of rugged terrain, the Manitoba Department of Highways has cleverly allowed potholes to breed and proliferate. This is likely a project undertaken in concert with the Department of Tourism to afford the traveler a multisensory experience. The sides of the highway furnish rugged sights of blasted, jagged stone, and the potholes generate the feel of the bone-jarring, pounding of the vehicle and the sounds of the crash, bang, and rattle of anything not bolted down.

Homophobia Part 2

When I had been traveling with the queers, we parted company south of Selkirk because they had planned to go south and travel through the United States. I declined to go with them and, truth be told, was very glad to have a way to politely part company. I had ridden with them a good part of the previous day. We had driven until quite late when Larry reported that he had driven far enough and suggested they might sleep in the car. He asked if I was okay to sleep outside. I happily said that would be fine, and we pulled into a rest area in the middle of nowhere. I unloaded my gear and walked to a spot under a tree at the edge of a farmer's field and rolled out my sleeping bag.

Although I had found them to be pleasant enough as we drove together, and they were even generous enough to buy me a hamburger for supper, I was still not completely sure about my traveling companions. I crawled into my sleeping bag and zipped it up tightly under my chin. They slept in the car.

I was still pretty nervous and not about to fall asleep. I kept one eye on the car and made numerous defence and escape plans. I got up and picked up a chunk of a fallen limb to serve me as a club if needed. After another hour or so of worry, I carefully and quietly moved my gear and myself over the barbed wire fence and felt better that I would at least have the screek of the wire fence to warn me of any unwanted advances. I stared at the stars for a few more hours. Eventually, I fell asleep.

I woke up terrified! Heavy breathing tickled my ear. I could hear dreadful licking of lips and I panicked. In one motion, I unzipped the bag, grabbed up my club, and flailed behind me. I scared the hell out of a curious Hereford calf who kicked up her heels, stuck her tail straight up in the air, and galloped over to her mother who was lying not far away chewing her cud. I was glad nobody in the car was awake to see me attack the innocently inquisitive calf. I quickly moved my stuff to the rest area side of the fence. I realized at that point that I needed to relax and get some sleep sometime soon and that wasn't going to happen with my present companions. So when Larry and Tim told me of their plans to go through the States, I saw my chance. I told them I wanted to see northern Ontario, and they let me out.

I stood by the highway watching as they headed south, leaving me to follow the Trans-Canada, I ruminated over my first contact with homosexuals while I organised my pack by the side of the road, and stuck out my thumb.

Back to the Future

Donna and I were in the Land of Rocks: grey, green, pink, orange, black; more and more rocks. We spent the night at West Hawk Lake in Whiteshell Provincial Park on the eastern edge of Manitoba. We set up on a level spot and off we went to explore Manitoba's deepest lake (364 feet deep).

A meteorite was responsible for making a great big hole in the ground. Geologists tell us that the meteorite smashed into the granite of the Canadian Shield and the resulting explosion left the crater which eventually filled with water. We walked the scenic loop which took us past a granite outcrop which gives an indication of the birth of the crater and along a great sandy beach which makes it a lovely spot for swimmers and sunbathers.

There isn't much difference between the eastern Manitoba rocks and the western Ontario rocks, so it was no great event when we crossed the provincial border. We were now in eastern Canada. It is an odd thing that Canadians have such a peculiar notion of geography. I am convinced that very few citizens could name Winnipeg as the nearest city to the east–west center of the country. Almost nobody will say that Winnipeg is in central Canada; that "honour" is usually conferred on Ontario.

Well, *I* knew that Ontario was east of center. Here in eastern Canada there was no sign of spring yet. It was certainly still quite cool as we rejoined the Trans-Canada. By 9:00 a.m., we were in Kenora, which we discovered is the home of Huskie, the Giant Muskie.

"Huskie, the Muskie" is the nickname of a 40-foot-tall outdoor sculpture depicting a fish in Kenora's McLeod Park. He gained his name and slogan: *Husky, the Muskie says 'Prevent water pollution'* which was used in a contest. With a fish as their mascot does that make the residents Muskievites?

We fuelled up, shopped for groceries, and took the van in for a wheel alignment. I suspected that all the potholes were taking their toll on our steering. So while the van was in the shop, we took a walk around Kenora, bought a few postcards, and got some lunch. The most amazing thing I learned about Kenora was that in 1907 the Kenora Thistles won the Stanley Cup! I would rather have seen Kenora's former name, Rat Portage, on the cup. I think it would give the small town hockey team a more aggressive name than Thistles. Maybe the Rat Portage Muskrats?

We drove on to Dryden. Somewhere between Kenora and Dryden we passed an Ontario Provincial Policeman sitting in his car at the side of the highway. He put on his flashing lights and pulled us over to the side of the road to inform us that the two plastic lawn chairs strapped to the back of the van restricted the view of our license plate and that we had to remove them. Funny that the RCMP in Alberta had not noticed the chairs when we went through the safety check in Crowsnest Pass. I mentioned it to the OPP officer hoping he would relent and pointed out that the plate was clearly visible from anywhere but looking straight down at the chair seat, the position he had taken.

No luck. So I undid the chairs and moved them over to the other rear door, being fastidious about tying them on so that he might not find fault with the fastenings. I have always suspected that a career in police work might attract some people who enjoy bossing other people around. I also theorized that they have difficulty exercising common sense. This guy appeared to support my theory, or he was just bored.

We saw the Big Moose in Kenora and more scenery, which was pretty rocky, and drove on to Upsala, where we stayed overnight in a campground by a little lake that was surrounded by more rock. The next day we went on through some more rocky country to Thunder Bay. Yahoo, they had gardens! We toured the friendship garden and took a break to visit the conservatory, which was a delight after so much bleak scenery. They had tropical and desert gardens, but strangely enough, no rock gardens.

After our spring flower fix,(this was springtime number four) we again headed east. We stopped at the Terry Fox Centre and, although I had told youngsters about Terry Fox many, many times over the years, I still found it was quite moving to see the statue beside the highway. We talked about what a journey that must have been for a young man.

Terry Fox was just a 12-year-old kid learning to play basketball back in Coquitlam when I passed this way in 1970. It would be ten more years before he came here. This wasn't a remarkable place to most passers-by, but it stands out in my memory because somewhere around here is where I embarked on my career as a drug smuggler.

Getting Lucky

The drug smuggling started innocently enough somewhere along this part of the Trans-Canada Highway. In 1970, I had hiked until I found a straight stretch so I could be seen some time in advance to allow a decent place for a car to pull over. There wasn't much point in standing along the edge of a bend or on a causeway through a lake.

By the time I reached this point, I was suffering from a lack of sleep, too much sun, and was getting a nasty cough. I'd had a couple of short rides since parting company with the homosexuals and, generally feeling like a piece of crap, I had wandered along the highway for a couple of hours after having been dropped off. It was hot. I was tired and hungry and thirsty. I put down my pack, set out my cardboard sign, ate one of the buns and a bit of cheese I'd bought in town, and drank a bottle of pop to round out my lunch.

There were very few cars going by. I half-heartedly stuck out my thumb as they approached from time to time. I was beginning to wonder where I might camp for the night and dreaded the thought of the bugs out here. I knew as soon as the sun went down I was going to become the main guest at a feast, sort of like those characters in a great big soup pot in a cannibal village. I rolled a smoke, thankful that I had a fresh pack of tobacco and plenty of papers and matches.

When I worked in a logging camp on northern Vancouver Island the previous summer, I came to realize that one of the few benefits of cigarette smoking was that bugs, by and large, don't like cigarette smoke. I was on a crew of three chokermen and a riggingslinger, and I was the only smoker. Between turns, we stood amid the slash and, like dumb animals, waved our hemlock branches around to try to keep the bugs off. The worst days were when the sky was heavy and the air was close with a light drizzle either starting or stopping. There was that horrible whining sound from mosquitoes, and the nasty silent pinpricks on your neck and face from the no-see-ums. It became second nature to have a little green hemlock branch in our dirty wet cotton gloves constantly waving around by our heads.

Sometimes when a really big log was hooked up and we knew it was going to be a long, slow pull up to the landing, I would quickly roll a smoke, light up, and sit on a log or stump happy to rest but even more pleased to have a little respite from the bugs. The other guys would crowd in to stand in the smoke and there were certainly no complaints about second-hand smoke. Sometimes when we were all frantic with bugs, they would even offer to set my choker if I would roll a smoke and they could stand in the drift. All I had to do was have a smoke break!

That's what I was doing in the hot sun on the side of the road in western Ontario: enjoying a smoke break and thinking of those cool drizzly west coast mountains. I had my pack in front of me and my cardboard sign leaning against the front of the pack. My sign said, "Please?" (I was nothing if not polite.)

There wasn't much traffic and most of it was big trucks.

A big truck should have been the perfect ride for a hitchhiker. They had lots of room for a pack, there was seldom a passenger; they went a long way at a stretch, and they even went at night. Unfortunately, most truck drivers had very little use for hitchhikers. In fact, many of them treated kids by the side of the road as a source of amusement or a target for their abuse. On more than one occasion I had been startled by a roaring air horn, or dusted off by a tractor-trailer that swerved very close to the shoulder where I was standing, or simply given the "Trudeau salute" by an obnoxious driver. I wasn't getting my hopes up for any of the big trucks that paraded by. However, hitchhiking is a lot like fishing. You never know when you might get a bite. I was hoping my luck might take a turn for the better when a little blue Volkswagen Beetle came around the bend. But when that Beetle got close enough to see the people inside, I figured there were two chances of it stopping: slim and none. The driver was a young blonde woman and the passenger was a little blonde girl. Not much chance of a ride there.

But, you never know. When I heard the change in that whirring buzz that a Volkswagen exhaust makes as it gears down, I didn't know what to make of it. When I saw the turn signal start to blink, I began to think I might actually get a ride. I still figured it was quite a longshot, but I ran up to the side of the car as the little girl rolled down the window. When the driver leaned forward and looked over to ask if I wanted a lift to the next town, I gave my most polite, "Yes, please."

I sat in the back along with my pack, biding my time. We introduced ourselves and I learned that

Diana was the driver and Rosie was her daughter. I didn't learn much else except that Rosie was six years old. Most of the conversation was more of an interrogation as Diana asked me about my destination, my home, my family, my studies, my trip so far, what plans I had for the rest of my trip, and so on. A break came when Rosie asked me if I wanted some of her animal crackers. Happily, I held out my hand and Rosie poured out an elephant, two giraffes, and two lions. She asked if she could have the elephant back because elephants were her favourites. So Rosie ate the elephant and I ate the giraffes and the lions.

As the miles went by, the interrogation eased off and I found out that they were from Calgary (I had noted the Alberta plates on the car), where Diana was a schoolteacher and Rosie was going to grade one in the fall, and Rosie's dad didn't live with them anymore. I suppose after her questioning, Diana didn't figure I was too much of a risk because as we approached the next town, she said that they could give me a ride a little further if I wanted. I wasn't about to decline.

Rosie informed me that they were camping and wanted to know if I was camping, too. When I told her that I was, she wanted to know if my tent was in my pack. I told her I had no tent and she wanted to know what I did when it rained. They had camped in the rain one night and if you touched the side of the tent the rain would get in. I said I usually found a spot under cover to sleep if it looked like rain and that I had a piece of plastic in case I got stuck where there was no cover.

Diana told me that they were headed to Stratford, where they were going to spend the summer with some theatre types that she knew. She said that I was welcome to have supper with them if I wanted and that she planned to stop at a provincial park south of White River. We found a nice campsite by a lake and there was enough of a breeze to keep the bugs at bay. I got a fire going and Diana set up their tent while Rosie gave instructions. Diana cooked us some supper while Rosie and I tossed rocks in the water. After supper, Rosie and I did dishes and then the three of us sat around the campfire.

When Rosie was asleep, Diana brought out a bag of dope and rolled up a smoke. I was happy to share it with her. I was quite pleased with life sitting with my back against a log, well fed, stoned, and with lovely company to share a campfire and conversation. But my not having slept well since Saskatchewan took its toll and the next thing I knew I was covered with my sleeping bag and the sun was up.

I checked my watch and discovered it was 7:00, so I got up and started my day. I went to the washhouse and shaved around the edges of my beard and, feeling cleaned up; I made a fire and set a pot of water to boil. I went down to the lake with a hot cup of tea and waited for the girls to get up. I noticed some noise from the tent and glancing up I saw Diana emerge, her shirt unbuttoned. Evidently she wore no bra. Trying not to stare at her breasts, I quickly looked out across the lake, but I must say that was quite an eye-opener for me.

Rosie popped out of the tent and we busied ourselves with breakfast and packing up our gear. With everything stowed, Rosie said she wanted to sit in the back so after she was in the car, I climbed into the front and off we went. In an hour or so we fuelled up in Wawa; we were amazed at the number of hitchhikers piled up there. I was feeling very lucky and said so to Diana. She looked pleased as well and as we headed south she talked about the day's drive ahead.

She told me she planned to go into Michigan at Sault Ste. Marie and then back into Canada at the Port Huron/Sarnia crossing and asked would I like to go along that way. Hell, I would have gone along if she were headed for the moon! She asked if I had some sort of ID and I said, yes, I had a passport with me. It was probably overkill, as far as identification went, but I was proud of having got one the year before, and pleased to finally have a use for it. I was a little nervous about the border crossing, though, because my only other experience with border guards had not gone well.

When I was 15, I had run away from home with my best friend. Neither of us was happy with our home lives, although, in retrospect, the foster home of my pal was truly unpleasant for him and I was just a fed up teenager. We tried to go through the Peace Arch border crossing near Vancouver in hopes of finding an uncle in Seattle who would put us up. We left Canada, no problem, but were refused entry into the USA. So we went back. We were refused re-entry into Canada! So we were stuck in that little strip of real estate that is covered by the borderline on a map. We joked when we read, "May These Gates Never Be Closed" carved onto the Arch, because they certainly were closed to us. But after a little consideration of *the world's longest undefended border,* we slipped away from the customs building and hiked through a field and were back into Canada a few minutes later.

Crossing the border at Sault Ste. Marie went as smoothly as anyone could have wanted; I didn't even get to show off my passport. We just pulled up and answered questions about where we were headed and what our plans were. Rosie announced that we were camping and that we got to sleep outdoors, and even had a campfire. The guard smiled and wished us a pleasant visit. It was a lovely summer day and we had a very pleasant drive through Michigan. Rosie was excited when we drove over the Mackinac Bridge, which is about a mile and a half long and way up about 200 feet above the water. I was quite impressed myself.

The rest of the drive was unremarkable and we motored on all day with regular stops for necessities and one other stop, which, at the time seemed ordinary enough. Diana pulled into some little town for gas and made a phone call while Rosie and I got a snack. Then we drove on a secondary road to a farmhouse where Diana went in to pick up something for a friend. She came out with a paper grocery bag with some green onions sticking out the top and found a place for it in the trunk at the front. In retrospect, it was a good thing that I had no idea what was in that bag.

By and by, we pulled into the border crossing at Port Huron/Sarnia and it went pretty much the same way as the crossing earlier in the day. We looked like a typical young family on vacation, I suppose. We went through without a hitch. Diana drove on for about five minutes and pulled over and asked me to drive for a bit. I said sure and asked if she felt OK. She said she was a bit tired and she looked a bit jangled. I got behind the wheel and Diana lit a smoke and leaned her head back while I took us out of Sarnia toward London.

We headed northeast and Diana took the wheel again as evening approached. Our arrival in Stratford was another eye-opener for me, but quite a different sort of revelation from the glimpse of Diana's breasts.

We pulled into a quiet, tree-lined street and up to a beautiful old house. Diana and Rosie went up to the front door and I followed a couple steps behind. Rosie rang the doorbell and a man appeared and gathered them both into his arms. Eventually I was introduced to Diana's fiancé, Roger, which fractured my young heart. Then Diana ran to the car and got the mysterious paper grocery sack, which she presented to Roger who appeared delighted.

We ate a few melted cheese sandwiches and Rosie went to bed. Roger opened the bag and set the greens aside and held up a number of plastic bags filled with weed. He opened one of the baggies and proceeded to roll up, light, and pass around "a number." It wasn't long before I was offered a place to sleep on the sofa and Diana and her fiancé trotted off upstairs.

I lay there for a few minutes considering my brief and unwitting career as a drug-smuggler. Was I likely to have been left, "holding the bag" had things gone wrong at the border? What would be easier than for Diana to claim I was an unknown hitchhiker and had brought the bag of dope along?

Then I thought about my misguided and unrealized career as a Lothario. Here I thought I had died and gone to heaven when Diana had seemed so warm and friendly. That bubble had quickly burst. I shrugged and smiled to myself. Sometimes you get lucky and sometimes you don't.

Fast Forward...

On a map, Nipigon is kind of like the top of the hump of Lake Superior. It almost feels like it is downhill from there. We quit for the day and parked the Marmot van in a truck layover. They were easy to get along with and quite generous about us staying there, but it was a little noisy because some of the trucks kept their engines running and some were coming and going at all hours, but we slept through most of it and were happy to use the washrooms in the morning. They have pay showers—free if you fill up with fuel! No propane for the Marmot van, though, until Wawa—home of the Giant Goose.

Wawa! When we came round a bend and saw the Big Goose, it was like trick photography where a scene transforms to an earlier time. Just like that, my hitchhiking trip returned vividly to my memory. I spent far too long there on my return to the west in 1970.

I clearly recalled the long, long, lines of hairy, colourfully clad, smoking and joking hitchhikers stretching east and west. The troops of travellers must have lined the highway for at least a quarter-mile each way. The deal was that you walked to the end of the line and spent a few days there waiting for a ride. The townsfolk were not exactly welcoming, but I think we outnumbered them so they weren't too nasty. Little did they know we were at least as anxious as they were to part company with their town.

We stopped in at the Giant Goose/Visitor Centre and had a look at some campground brochures and talked to the helpful staff, which was a far warmer welcome that I had received the last time I was in Wawa. We stayed at the Wawa Resort and Campground in a great spot overlooking the river and were treated very well. I had a chance to get caught up with my emails and do a little searching about the road ahead. After supper, we stretched our legs a bit and enjoyed a peaceful night.

We slacked around the next morning and had quite a late start. We decided to go into town so we drove past the goose again and drove down Mission Road. It is lined with motels and various businesses which, unfortunately, all seem to have known better times. Young's General Store caught our eye because it was quite blatantly hokey-looking with a big museum quality stuffed moose; my kind of place. They had everything! It was a great place to browse, with clothes and souvenirs and jams and jellies, even a pickle barrel. It was an old wooden barrel with a flip-up lid, filled with cucumber pickles swimming in brine. Donna grabbed the tongs and fished out a couple of pickles for our lunch. There was an unusual selection of various fruit jams that she hadn't seen before so Donna loaded up. We fuelled up the van and headed back to the info centre. After we had our lunch there, with the zingiest pickles I've ever eaten, I decided to make some repairs to the driver's seat that I had installed back home. I wasn't happy with the position of the lumbar support, which is an inflatable cushion hooked into the seatback.

We got a few odd looks as I removed the bolts, pulled out the seat, flopped it onto a picnic table, and opened the seatback. I was able to unclip the cushion and move it down to where I wanted and refasten the clips. I was quite pleased with the result when it was back together. Mobile repairs all done, we headed for the highway junction.

I got a laugh out of Donna when I pointed out one lonely hitchhiker going the other way. He was dressed like the '70s with jeans and a buckskin coat, with long grey hair and whiskers. I told Donna that perhaps he was trapped in the time-space continuum and was still waiting for a ride after all these years...

The highway continues downhill on the map from Wawa to Sault Ste. Marie. I'm told that this part of the highway always has some sort of construction going on, but apart from the highways workers with their stop/slow signs and a few rough patches, the trip was okay.

My mother's side of the family is well represented in Sault Ste. Marie and area. We had the good fortune to meet some of the relatives and enjoy their hospitality as well as see some of the sights of the city. We even got a tour of city hall from the mayor himself. Both of my maternal grandparents had been born on farms in the area. We had thought of visiting the old places, but were disappointed to learn that the old buildings were gone and most of the land was overgrown.

After a couple nights' stay touring and visiting, we decided to say goodbye and carry on, eventually crossing over to Manitoulin Island to make connections with the ferry to the Bruce Peninsula.

It was a pleasant drive on a Sunday morning. We especially enjoyed the views where Highway17 follows the Missisagi River. We stopped for tea in a rest area by the river. The water was like a mirror and the reflection of the forest on the opposite bank was a delight. It is not hard to see how the scenery here in eastern Canada inspired the Group of Seven and many other Canadian artists.

We stopped in Espanola and had an early lunch, then took Highway 6 south across Manitoulin Island. We looked for a campground when we neared the ferry landing and found a place on the shore where we stayed overnight. We had time for a brisk walk along the shore of Lake Huron, and because the weather was turning a bit nasty, we wore our coats and hats. That night quite a storm blew in with terrible thunder and lightning all night. It was windy and cold out!

Ferry on Lake Huron

In the morning, we paid $60.00 and took the wallowing ferry across Lake Huron/Georgian Bay to the Bruce Peninsula. Not a happy experience. It was an ugly old boat and there were grey skies and wind and rain all the way. The cafeteria was pretty much what we were used to on BC Ferries: vague food and crowded quarters. The viewing decks held no attraction on such a miserable weather day, so we sat in the lounge area for a while then wandered to the gift shop and back. After a bit I went to find a bathroom and discovered that the toilets operate on some sort of vacuum system and make a noise like an underwater monster. I heard a youngster report to his dad that the noise scared the crap out of him.

The first ferry on our current trip, from Nanaimo to Vancouver, was on a special fare ($45.30), so it seemed less unpleasant than usual, although the noxious "ferry food" is always a danger. We braved a snack and some juice in the cafeteria. With the whole of Canada stretched out before us, our excitement about our trip negated the usual tedium of a ferry ride. I suppose the first time across is interesting, but I have been travelling that route since the late 1950s and the novelty has pretty much worn off.

The second, a free ferry from Needles to Fauqier in B.C.'s Kootenays, was actually as near to perfect as a ferry ride can be. It's interesting in that there is a cable across the bottom of the lake and looking over the side, a passenger can watch the ferry spool along the line as it travels across the lake. Add to that the fact that the Needles ferry ride has a perfect duration to maintain the excitement of a voyage: it's a 5-minute crossing. Sadly, Needles is actually a misnomer because the damming of the Columbia River drowned Needles in the 1960s. I understand that what used to be the town lies somewhere under the water.

The third, the longest free ferry ride in the world, was a 40 minute scenic crossing of Kootenay Lake from Balfour to Kootenay Bay, B.C..

The free ferries were a wonderful experience. You just drive up and wait until you load on and go. The inland ferries operate under private contract with the Ministry of Transportation and Infrastructure. The sign at the dock read ALL INLAND FERRIES ARE FREE OF CHARGE TO USERS. Unfortunately, this government magnanimity does not extend to the coastal regions of the province. We islanders only have pay ferries.

I have long believed that the right-wing voters of BC's interior are well served because of their support for the variously named right-wing provincial governments that have held power for more than 50 of the last 65 years. We Islanders tend to elect left-wing representatives and don't enjoy the same beneficence as our fellow citizens on the mainland. But we fight the good fight and we grudgingly pay to take the ferry.

After a couple of hours on the *MS Chi-Cheemaun*, we were very happy to disembark at the Tobermory terminal on the Bruce Peninsula. We followed Highway 6 south through the northern part of the peninsula to Wiarton. We stopped in to visit Wiarton Willie, the most famous groundhog in Canada and the only albino weather prognosticator in the world. Wiarton Willie's prediction of the timing of spring is a news event that captures the interests of people around the world. Smarmy was pretty thrilled to meet this memorable meteorological marmot.

We then headed south along the east coast of Lake Huron. As the day progressed, the weather steadily improved.

We ended the day in a great campground near Kincardine on the shore of Lake Huron. The people there were very hospitable and once we signed in, led us right to our spot. The campsite was just what I like; there were mature hedges affording privacy to the comfortable, level sites. The water was good and our picnic table was just right to enjoy our supper. In the evening, we went for a leisurely stroll down to the shore and tossed some stones into the huge lake. In the morning, the showers were clean and the water was hot. All in all, top marks from me!

We drove south along the shore on Highway 21. The countryside was alive with springtime. Newly tilled fields and lush green pastures were such a pleasant change from the bleak Canadian Shield. Farmers were hard at it everywhere we looked and we realized that in this area farming must have been a far more lucrative endeavour than in the northern and western parts of Ontario where we had been. We were also interested to see a lot of wind turbines, presumably generating electricity. Before we knew it, we were in the "Prettiest Town in Canada."

At least that is what the residents of Goderich claim. I have to admit that if I were picking, Goderich would be right up there. The town layout is interesting in itself because the centre is an octagon. If you look at a map, the octagon is situated at the centre of a square, creating a web of streets. We went to the centre and drove around the octagon once, then parked and set out on foot for some shopping and sightseeing.

Donna managed to find a quilters' shop and I left her to her own devices while I went in search of a bakery. Touring around for a while, I found a purveyor of muffins and loaded up. I sampled one while I retraced my steps to the quilt shop. Wiping the guilty crumbs from my whiskers, I went in and found Donna finishing up her shopping. We took a leisurely drive around town, oohing and ahhing over the heritage homes on our way to see the Huron Historic Gaol.

I sent this message home on a postcard:

Did time in gaol in Goderich. They have a restored gaol from the 1800s. Not a place you want to be incarcerated. Escaped at lunch.

In the jail, we took a look at the cells, which were anything but fun. They were small and dark and likely cold to stay in. The great, thick, whitewashed walls were only interrupted by steel doors and tiny barred windows at the end of shafts cut into the walls. We went up to the top floor, which was set up as a courtroom. From the austere furnishings, it wasn't hard to see how justice might have been meted out. By the looks of things, the treatment there was, if not harsh, then at the least very serious business.

We were intrigued with the Governor's House, which was attached to the southeast side of the Gaol. With its dark ash woodwork, ornate oak furnishings, velvet drapes and lace curtains, it wasn't hard to imagine that the governor's position was a pretty important one in the early part of the 20th century. The relative luxury of his home, built to house the governor and his family, is a stark contrast to the harsh conditions endured by the prisoners only a few feet away. Better to be the hammer than the nail!

During the tour, Donna and a guide talked about the kitchen and I wandered off to the cells. I learned from one of the museum staff that the gaol and courthouse were still in use until 1972. As I stood imagining being locked up in one of the cells, a feeling like a cold wind shivered through me. I realized that in 1970, I had been very, very close to being locked up in that gaol. And the whole incident could be traced to the misunderstanding of one word.

You see, where I grew up, a "case of beer" meant a cardboard box with a handle in the top, and it held twelve bottles. However, as I was to learn, in that part of Ontario, to speak of a "case of beer" was to describe a carton holding 24 bottles. So instead of a couple cases of beer meaning 24 bottles, it meant 48. And with 48 bottles of beer on a Saturday night, three farm boys could get into all sorts of trouble with the law. Which we did.

Farm Boys

As you can imagine, for a disappointed teenager, the shine went off Stratford pretty fast once I realized I didn't figure very prominently in Diana's plans, so I thanked my host in the morning and headed for the highway. When I saw the name Goderich on my map, I remembered Shorty. I met Shorty in a logging camp at Port McNeill on the north end of Vancouver Island the summer earlier. He and I were not great friends, but in the way of logging camp drinking acquaintances, we had shared stories about growing up. That is how I came to know that Shorty had grown up on a farm "near Goderich." That was also how I came to have a standing invitation to visit if I was "ever to get out that way." Like a good Boy Scout, I had anticipated such a situation by putting Shorty's address and phone number in my address book.

I made a call and learned that Shorty was still out west in a logging camp somewhere, but Shorty's dad said I was welcome to come and stay for a few days if I liked. That was good enough for me, so I wrote down the directions he gave me and thumbed my way out of Goderich into farming country. I arrived at the farm late in the afternoon. Shorty's dad showed me a room where I could put my stuff and asked if I had been on a farm before. He was very pleased when I said that I had some farm experience and knew how to milk cows.

"Good," he said, "then you can help with the chores if you like."

We fed the pigs and chickens and gathered the eggs. They had only one gentle old Jersey milk cow and Shorty's dad leaned against a post beside the stall and talked as I sat down and milked. By the time I was done, I learned that Shorty was the youngest (therefore the name Shorty) and the last one to leave home. The old man ran the place by himself, being a widower for some years, although Shorty's brother Bill came home on weekends from his job in a nearby town to help out. This being Thursday, if I wanted to stay and help with the pigs on Friday, I could meet Bill the next evening. Over a big meal of fried potatoes, ham, and beans, I was made to feel as welcome as could be and felt that I could come to like Shorty's dad. I washed up the dishes and we took our tea out to the porch where we smoked and talked about the west coast and farming and logging. I was glad to have a chance to brag about my part of the country, although I could see that there was a little skepticism on Shorty's dad's face when I talked about big trees that were six to eight feet through. He said Shorty had told him about those big trees, but added that Shorty had always been inclined to BS a little. I left it at that.

When I went up to my room for the night I felt right at home and slept very contentedly indeed.

Next morning over a big bowl of oatmeal, I learned we were going to move some hay bales in the morning and "cut pigs" after lunch. Moving hay bales is not too technical and the job went without a hitch.

Over lunch I had to admit that I had never "cut pigs," but was assured that I would get to do the easy part. Shorty's dad would do the tricky part, and the dog would do the other part. I was given a pair of leather gloves, some coveralls, and a pair of rubber boots that more or less fit.

OK, time to cut pigs.

The easy part turned out to be a series of parts: going in to a pen full of the little squealers; grabbing a young pig by the hind leg and lifting it off the concrete and muck; carrying the writhing, screaming, flailing, little porker by the hind feet over to a bale of hay in the alley of the barn; then, like a football centre, hiking the pig back through my legs onto the hay bale so it landed on its back; and finally, sitting on it while holding its hind legs tightly so it couldn't kick and jump. All the while the pig was screaming like a banshee, completely convinced we were going to murder it.

The tricky part turned out to be quite quick. Shorty's dad cut a slit in the pig's scrotum, popped out its testicles, and snipped them off. Even quicker was the dog's part. He ate the testicles.

There were about 20 pigs in that pen. By the time we were done, I was as tired as a Turkish wrestler, covered in pig shit, and my own testicles had suffered more than once while fighting the unruly little swine. At least now I could add cutting pigs to my resume.

I had a shower and got cleaned up while Shorty's dad made supper. Before we sat at the table, Shorty's brother Bill arrived. Bill and I hit it off right away. Bill had been slated to help with the pigs the next day. He was really glad that he didn't have to cut pigs, and I was happy when Bill invited me along to go out for the evening. We ate our fill and Shorty's dad wished us well as we climbed into Bill's red and white '67 Impala.

It was when we drove to Bill's buddy's place that I learned that Bill had a case of beer; and his buddy Dan was to bring along another case. I offered to chip in for the beer, but Bill said that by helping cut the pigs I had contributed more than enough. It was when I saw Dan packing 24 bottles of beer that I asked about and learned the eastern definition of a case of beer. Well, at least we weren't likely to run out. Dan and I were introduced over the first of the 48 beers.

Bill and Dan filled me in on the program for the evening as we drove. There was a dance in a town about half an hour away and the girls in that town were reputed to be friendly and fun-loving, especially if there was plenty of beer around. Not only had my companions scouted out a likely venue to meet friendly girls, but they had also procured enough beer to ensure the success of their plan. As I drank my second beer, it seemed that I had taken up with a couple of smooth operators and it promised to be a great night.

We parked the Impala, had a smoke, and opened another beer. We figured to dance for a while, scout out the available members of the opposite sex, and eventually invite a few of the girls along for a party at the lake. After finalizing the plan, we stubbed out our smokes, knocked back the beers, and tossed the empty bottles into the brush. We went to the hall's entrance, paid, and sauntered into the dance. Things went like clockwork. There were indeed fun-loving girls all over the place. Bill was our star player. He was a big strapping fellow about six-foot two with dark hair and a winning smile. Dan was a little smaller and not as outgoing, but teamed with Bill he did all right. I, on the other hand, felt a bit out of place at first, but with some alcohol-induced confidence and a winning smile from a curly-haired girl named Suzie, was soon having a swell time, too.

It didn't take long at all to gather up our newfound partners and slip out to the Chev. We were smoking and joking and having a beer in the parking lot with these great girls when some of the local lads took exception to our visit to their territory. Instead of our little group having a few drinks and a few laughs, the atmosphere quickly turned stormy. It was rudely suggested that we go home. I then learned that Dan had a short temper and an inflammatory manner of speaking. He offered an insult to a like-minded fellow from the other side and punctuated his observation with a poke in the nose. A couple of the boys immediately wanted to take a round out of Dan and he was eager to oblige. Bill wasn't shy either and waded right in, and in a blink, I was drawn into the scuffle as well by somebody who grabbed me by the shoulder and clipped me on the side of the head with his fist.

It was a little different from my afternoon with the pigs in that these guys wanted to hit me, but on the bright side, there was a lot less squealing and it was easier to move without wearing oversize gumboots. However, before much fighting really happened, we heard a yell that somebody had called the cops, and the other combatants disappeared like rats down a sewer drain. We bailed into the car and left. I remember seeing a demure little wave from Suzie as we tore out of the parking lot.

As Bill explained as we made our getaway, the cops knew his car, and if we got caught with the beer there would be hell to pay. Dan then explained that he and Bill had been in some trouble with the cops before and there was nothing those cops would like better than to toss the three of us into the county jail. (The one in Goderich, remember?) As if to make his point, a police car whined up the street after us with no interest at all in the parking lot we had just left. I felt the bruise on the side of my head and worried about the cops. Through the haze of a few beers, the nasty picture of a night in jail began to emerge.

JAIL! The can, the clink, the cooler, the joint, the slammer, stir, up the river, the crowbar hotel. Yep, bread and water, mean and cruel guards, probably a hanging judge. I didn't want to go to jail. I was beginning to fear the worst with those police after us, but lucky for me, Bill and Dan had a plan for this turn of events as well.

"Don't worry," said Dan, opening fresh beers, "we have a plan."

The first part of the plan was to drive really, really, fast. Bill was executing that part. That Chev was quite a fast car. It was one of the few cars I have ridden in with a 427 cubic inch engine. When Bill stood on the accelerator pedal, it growled. It was a good thing I was drunk, or I might have gotten nervous as I watched the speedometer climb. Bill was a good driver though, and was doing a great job. He kept his beer between his legs for the turns and twists and only drank on the straightaways.

Dan told me his part of the plan was to really piss off the cops, as he held up his empty beer bottle, leaned out of the window, and tossed it back towards the cop car. "It's good I can throw left- handed," he reported, taking another empty from Bill. Although the fast driving might have given the cops enough reason to be after us, I believe to this day that tossing the beer bottles at them was what really motivated them to catch us. Like poking a stick in a beehive or waving a red flag at a bull, Dan was masterful at doing his part and kept those cops riled up.

I could see that both Bill and Dan were executing their parts perfectly, but I still failed to see how the outcome of this chase could be good in any way. I did notice that Bill had been taking twists and turns to less and less traveled roads and we were now barrelling down a dirt road with the Chev throwing up clouds of dust like a volcanic plume behind us. The cop car was somewhere back in that dust wailing impotently. Then the road emptied into a gravel pit; there were just two tracks in front of us. This looked like a dead end to me as we slowed a bit and I began to envision life in prison again, but before I could dwell on those thoughts, Dan began to cackle and congratulate Bill who was grinning broadly. The dust had died down a bit and the police car closed up on us a little. I felt left out of the joke. I was going to ask one of the guys what they were grinning about when everything went weird.

The engine roared for a sec and then the car was suddenly quite quiet. Time stopped. I could see nothing in front of us. We just sailed through the dark slowly tilting down at the nose a bit and then a big whump! A bounce or two and we were on our way up a steep track out of the pit. I turned in time to see the police car brake hard behind us and start to slide towards the edge of the three-foot bank that we had just flown off. The cop car was barely stopping in time. Slowly, it slid up to the edge, turning sideways a little, coming to a halt before the edge of the bank. The siren's wail petered out behind us.

"Hot damn! That calls for a beer!" announced Dan, and all three of us grinned like fools.

Now that was a plan! A pretty crazy plan, but magnificent in its final execution. I believe that was one of the wildest rides I have ever been on. The only really disconcerting bit was leaving the girls behind at the dance.

Even basking in the glory of his success, Bill kept his head. Knowing that the cops had radios, he drove sedately into the next town and up the street where his granny lived. Granny's house was an older two-storey place with its garage in the basement so you could simply drive down into it from the street, which is what we did. Bill informed us that Granny was as deaf as a post and wouldn't even know we were there as we parked in her basement, closed the garage door, and doused all the lights. He was right.

We sat out on the back porch and smoked and drank most of the night away, delighting in the remembered details of out night out. I was sleeping on the porch swing when Bill woke me up early in the morning and the three of us eased the car out of Granny's basement and went home.

In Norse mythology the three Norns are the goddesses of fate and they spend their time spinning the threads of life and weaving a tapestry of the destinies of all living beings. When I left Goderich I was a little the worse for wear but happily, when the Norns spun my fate, a stay at that "gaol" was not included.

The Falls

Donna interrupted my jailhouse reverie and suggested we get back on the road. So we left Goderich and its jail behind and made our way to Stratford. I told Donna that I remembered Stratford as being a picturesque little town that was easy to get around. But when we arrived in mid-afternoon, we got caught up in road construction with its usual mess and machinery, and a detour that caused us to take a long time to make our way downtown to look for the info centre. We spotted it, pulled into the parking lot and, to our dismay, we found pay parking! We forked out some coin and then, to add insult to injury, the info centre door was shut! We checked the time and thought it was a pretty early closing for the day. Further investigation revealed that the centre wouldn't actually open for the season until the next week. Once again no regrets about leaving Stratford.

Moving on, we drove southeast on Highway 6, then east to a great little campground just off Highway 17. The place was run by some really nice people, who got us set up for the night. We made the most of the hot showers and had a nice quiet, restful night. This was a good thing because we were headed for the wild and crazy town of Niagara Falls tomorrow.

The next morning we stopped for a silly photo op on the highway posing in front of the Woodstock sign. Peace signs and all - Far Out Man!

Then, totally out of character, we saddled up the Marmot van and drove on the 403 freeway to Niagara Falls. The highway was busy, but we got where we wanted to go. By that point, we had had our fill of secondary roads with their crop of potholes from the previous winter(s).

We stopped in Saint Catharine's and were amazed when we came to a bridge over the Welland Canal. We were about fourth or fifth in line and watched as the bridge went up and a freighter went across in front of us. It was huge and looked like it was driving on a cross street. We decided to see more of the canal after Niagara Falls.

The town of Niagara Falls looks like a cross between Las Vegas and Disneyland. It was a monument to the occupation of separating tourists from their money. When I was a boy, we would often travel to fairs and exhibitions with our 4-H projects and invariably would be lured by the siren call of the midway. It didn't take long to learn that unless you had a pretty girl on your arm and there was a good-sized crowd around, you could never win the stuffed toy. Niagara Falls had that same feel about it. It was too wild for us, so we kept our heads down and drove on through to the park.

We were ushered into an enormous parking lot and then, with Smarmy and Charlotte and our camera, we set out to explore....The Falls

We were not disappointed. It was amazing. I couldn't get enough of the views. Like excited kids, we stuck our heads over the rails and walked in the spray, and posed and asked strangers to take our pictures, and posed Smarmy and Charlotte and took their pictures, and looked down at the Maid of the Mist (and gave up on the lineup for the Maid of the Mist), and disparaged the falls on the USA side as sour grapes anyhow.

Instead we chose "Journey Behind the Falls." Here is a bit of history from their website:

In 1903, a tunnel was built behind the Horseshoe Falls with a connecting elevator to transport employees that worked at the power generating station at the base of the Falls. In 1924, an extension was built over 50 metres long under the Horseshoe Falls, and over time additions such as electricity and a protected tunnel lined in concrete were built. It wasn't until 1951 that an outdoor observation platform was constructed, and today we have the "Journey Behind the Falls" scenic attraction as it looks today.

We took the elevator down under the falls and were awestruck at the noise and power of the water. We put on the funny yellow raincoats and got wet anyhow. The views and the spray made for a complete sensory experience. Sadly, a group of teenaged schoolgirls arrived at the observation deck a little while after we did. Evidently they were unsupervised and totally lacking in any social graces. They drove us out with their shrieking and cacophonous banter. To add insult to injury, a few barged their way into the loaded elevator with us to make our ride back up unpleasant. A fellow passenger, an elderly woman, finally scolded them for being inconsiderate and they went quiet. Before they got off, they meekly apologized. The peace and tranquility of the gardens up top revived us a little, but sitting still, we realized we were getting tired and hungry so we went back to the van and made a late lunch.

After a rest, we bade the falls farewell and went to visit the Welland Canal. We drove down the Welland Canal Parkway and found a spot where we could stop and look over Lock 5. The lock itself was isolated by a chain link fence, but there was lots of room to park and the place was pleasantly quiet after the throngs at the falls. The canal was fascinating; we watched a ship approach and enter the lock. At the same time, a minivan pulled up and a family climbed out. They were evidently saying goodbyes. The little ones were saying goodbye to grandpa by the looks of it, and then the young family got back in the van and Grandpa picked up his kitbag and came and stood by the gate near us.

Because he looked like he knew his way around, I asked him if he could tell me a bit about the lock. He was happy to oblige. He turned out to be a steersman for the lake freighters we were looking at and was getting back on his ship at the lock after having spent some leave with his son and family. His ship had dropped him off on the way upstream and he was going to rejoin the crew for the trip down.

We were fascinated by his talk and listened for a couple of minutes while he outlined the nature of the ships and how they passed through the locks. They have only twenty-odd feet to spare end-to-end to fit in the locks, and only a foot or two side-to-side. While he spoke, his ship slid in and stopped opposite us.

The steersman managed to get the attention of a passing worker inside the fence and explained that he wanted to go aboard. The worker in turn radioed and a uniformed official came in a golf cart to see what he wanted. The worker nodded and went on his way. The steersman explained what he wanted to the uniformed woman but, unfortunately, she had not brought the key to the gate. He was not impressed. Meanwhile, the ship was beginning to rise and he said that once it got so high it would be a tough job to get on. What he wanted was to simply step aboard as the deck of the ship came up level with the lock and would she please get the key without delay.

We watched impotently as the ship continued to rise and the woman in uniform drove away in her golf cart. After having given such an eloquent discourse about the nature of ships and locks and canals, our steersman now began quite a revealing diatribe about the canal employees in general and our woman in uniform in particular. It seems he didn't have a high regard for her ingenuity nor her competency. It proved to be a fair assessment.

Time being of the essence, I offered to help. I moved beside the gate and bent forward and wove my fingers together to make a stirrup above my knee. Our steersman placed his foot on my palms and, with a bit of grunting and struggling by each of us, we got him over the fence. I tossed his bag over to him and wished him well as he hurried the 50 feet or so to the ship and just managed to get aboard. In only a matter of minutes, we were staring up at a wall of more than 30 feet of sheer red hull as the ship towered above us. It was then that the woman with the key returned and when she asked where our steersman was I pointed up to the deck of the ship.

That evening, we met my cousins who live near Hamilton. We were warmly welcomed, had a lovely meal, and a delightful evening getting to know each other. The girls are both quilters and they shared projects while I got to compare notes on gardening and hockey. Donna asked about the Royal Botanical Gardens in Burlington and we were assured they were well worth a visit, so we planned to stop in the next morning.

After breakfast, we checked our maps, thanked our hosts amid promises to keep in touch, and continued on our expedition.

The gardens were great. We were there early and had the place pretty much to ourselves. At this point in the trip, it was a real tonic to explore the plantings. The prairies and northern Ontario have their own charm, but we realized how much we liked the scents and scenes of beautiful gardens. Spring flowers number 5 for us

Two things stand out about the gardens, both related to my former life as a schoolteacher. In the magnificent Rock Garden, there was an enormous, gnarly old tree, which I immediately recognized as Old Man Willow in Tolkien's *Lord of the Rings*. I had to tell Donna about reading that passage to my class back in the late '70s and the tag game of Old Man Willow we made up. My granddaughter tells me the kids at her school still play that game. I just had to take a picture.

The second was the Lilac Walk. The lilacs were a delight to both the eyes and the nose, and while we strolled along we met several classes of primary students on an outing. Some were drawing, some writing about their visit, some working with guides, and one group sat out of the sun around a teacher reading a picture book. Since I had retired, that was the first time I missed having a bunch of kids for story time. I was tempted to hip-check the teacher and take over the reading—but only for a second.

Near the end of our visit, Donna and I sat on a bench overlooking a formal garden when it occurred to me that I would like a picture of the two of us. There was a fellow standing nearby and I asked him, as millions of tourists ask people every day, if he would please take a picture of us with our camera. He was very obliging and quite fastidious about getting a good shot, even posing us just right. We thanked him for his efforts and with a big smile he said that he liked to do a good job. As he gave me back my camera, he handed me his business card. Happily, we learned that he was a portrait photographer who was visiting the gardens to plan a wedding shoot. Some days you do get lucky...

Soon we were faced with the prospect of driving through Toronto or taking secondary roads around the city. By now you know I have an aversion to driving in city traffic, in fact, to driving in big cities in general. This runs contrary to the aim of roadbuilders, of course. I call it my Rome theory: 2000 years ago in Europe, the centre of commerce and power was Rome, hence the quote, "All roads lead to Rome" and most roads did. Present day politicians and those who finance them are usually city-dwellers and all of them reckon their city is the new Rome, so all major roads lead to it. This is certainly the case for Toronto. If you want to go *to* Toronto, there are lots and lots of signs to lead you and tell you how far it is. However, if you want to go *away* from Toronto (and who would ever want to go away from Toronto?) you're on your own. Avoiding Toronto requires lots of map reading and exploring secondary highways.

The good news is that since major highways don't offer the opportunities to sightsee and visit that are afforded by roads less travelled, we got a chance to see a bit more of Ontario, which turned out to be very interesting and enjoyable. We ended the day camped beside the Rideau Canal near Smith Falls. We had stopped in at an unusually good infocentre/museum and learned that the canal is set up for recreational boaters. There are lock stations for hikers, cyclists, and boaters to stay overnight, complete with public facilities. When we asked if RVers (us) might make use of one of the overnight stops, the girl thought for a minute and then said "Well, usually not, but it's early in the season so the lockmaster might let you if nobody is using it."

The lock station turned out to be quite interesting. The locks were still operated by the original hand-driven mechanisms, which we investigated. A big hand crank opened and closed the lock gates and gravity and buoyancy did the rest. The station itself was located on a hill at the narrow end of an expanse of water teeming with birds and frogs. We went across a bridge over the canal and up a rise to the station and talked to the lockmaster for a while. He filled us in on life at a lock station and a bit of history as well. As is often the case, the lockmaster wanted to hear about our travels so far and what it was like on our island, and what it was like island-hopping in our old wooden boat. It was a very pleasant visit for an hour or so. Feeling like we were in the company of a kindred soul, we asked if we might stay the night in the parking lot and use the facilities; we were warmly welcomed to do so. We settled in for the night listening to the frogs and loons. In the morning, we got cleaned up at the station and left a thank-you for the delightful stay. We congratulated ourselves for giving Toronto a wave.

The next day we went as far as Cornwall and, because I was feeling a little poorly, camped early and took it easy for most the day. It was a warm, sunny afternoon and we went exploring along the docks at the marina, checking out the boats. Back at the campground after supper, we speculated about our U.S. neighbours in New York state across the river.

Well, It's A Long Way From Hope

I am making notes in a provincial park just inside the New Brunswick border. It's a kind of refuge from Quebec. I like to try to decipher French as much as the next guy, but it is a little overwhelming after a few days. The Quebecers have been great, but they do speak fast. The capper was this morning when I spent 5 minutes struggling to explain that the propane tank on the Marmot van had an automatic shutoff, that I would like the tank filled, and that it would likely take about 40 litres. The attendant was very patient and coached me through my halting speech. After he finished filling the tank, he turned to me and said, in English, "Well, that about does it for the propane. That'll be thirty-six, forty-five, please." It inspires humility when the guy pumping gas is so much more competent at communication than I am.

Donna's aunt and uncle in Montreal had planned a visit to the west coast and we arrived at the outskirts of the city the day after they had departed, so we decided to try to slip south of the city and pretty much give it a wide berth, as we had for Toronto. Like Toronto, it was a challenge. I developed a second theory in addition to my Rome theory. I call it my Mecca theory: the faithful, I am told, face Mecca to pray no matter where they are. Well, road signs near a large city are similar. They can be depended upon to tell you where you are if you're facing the city, but if you're facing away it, is much more difficult to get your bearings. This probably means nothing to those who have a satellite navigation system in their vehicle, but for those of us who still make use of paper roadmaps, useful highway signs are a boon.

Besides starting an immersion course in French near Montreal, we were also able to observe a new kind of driver. We had seen lots of different kinds of drivers so far on our trip, but near Montreal we met a new species that was totally unlooked-for. Both Donna and I were taken by surprise several times by this unusual hybrid. It seems Montreal has a species of driver that is equally at home behind the wheel of a school bus or a NASCAR race car. I believe there must be a driving school with a name like "Mario Andretti's School of Bus Driving" somewhere in Montreal. In any case, I certainly wasn't prepared for huge yellow vehicles darting around like sports cars. Other bus drivers are mere go-cart racers compared to these school bus types. I always thought of a school bus's yellow colour as defensive: other drivers should easily see the buses and take extra care to obey the rules of the road. With Montreal's school buses, the yellow colour means "These drivers play offense"

An hour and a half later on the Trans-Canada, we pulled into a big campground near Drummondville. It was a source of lots of new experiences for us. For starters, it was devoted to seasonal sites, which suggests that they are there for the whole summer season, but in actuality, they are there year-round. People acquire a site and set up their trailer for years and years. We saw little gardens and rockeries and lawn furniture and ornaments and barbecues just like a cottage someplace. The guys in the site next to us had a lawn swing fashioned like an old carriage. The whole campground was like a cute little village.

The toilets were a bit different from what we were used to. They were set up here and there like outhouses, with the doors facing the roads. They didn't have full doors and there was at least a foot or more gap at the bottom. I suppose that was so you could easily see if the toilet was occupied, or if you were inside you could get plenty of fresh air and bugs. It was a bit weird, though, to have your trousers around your ankles for the world to see.

The highlight of our stay was supper at the cabaña canteen. It was warm and cozy and friendly and almost like having supper camping with friends. Our table was in a screened porch. We could see over a counter into the kitchen and the whole place was kind of summer-camp-rustic. I had my first taste of poutine, sort of like chips and gravy and cottage cheese, which I found quite tasty and filling. I always have room for dessert, so I tried *tarte au sucre*. That maple sugar pie seemed harmless enough, but it was like trying soft drugs. It was delightful and, apparently, harmless. That's how you get hooked, of course. It just seems like safe fun at first. The maple syrup memory stayed with me all night. The next day I got a half-litre can of maple syrup at the local grocery and poured a little over some of those small cake donuts at lunch. I tried some more at supper, some for a snack in the evening, and finished off the can on my pancakes for breakfast. I got a whole litre can later that day and tried dipping donuts in a saucer of syrup, or pouring some in my tea and all over ice cream or on pie... It's that old sad story, a slippery slope downhill to addiction. Before I knew it, I was a can-a-day user. I had that maple syrup monkey on my back.

We wanted to visit Quebec City but the idea of driving in the city and finding parking with the Marmot van was daunting. We lucked out with some advice from one of the waitresses at the campground who told us about parking on the other side of the St. Lawrence River in Levis, and taking the passenger ferry across the river. We easily found plenty of parking and slipped across on the ferry for a day trip.

The old city was nothing like anything I had seen before. It really was something to ponder its age, standing in a 400 year-old street. I am not a city person, but for a change of pace Samuel de Champlain's capital city really is worth a look. Who knew back in the beginning of the seventeenth century that this would turn out so well? We walked around the lower town on the cobblestone streets and marvelled at the buildings, which sported plaques showing the dates they were built, and then took the funicular to the upper town to see the Chateau Frontenac.

The funicular is a cross between an elevator and a train. It is steep. The trip on the line travels 210 feet up at a 45-degree angle. In 2004, the funicular celebrated 125 years of service. At the top, we toured around, did some shopping, and looked for a good, cheap lunch. We picked the wrong place and got a bad, expensive lunch, but we found some swell moose-shaped maple sugar suckers (I was onto the hard stuff now). We also got tired feet, and some verbal abuse from a driver who was unhappy about me crossing the street against the light, which I had failed to notice. Like Candide I took his outburst as an opportunity. I did get a chance to increase my french vocabulary.

We checked out a "tourist highlight" but found we were too late for the early show and too early for the later re-enactment of the battle of the Plains of Abraham. We were getting quite tired and didn't want to wait for the late one, so we looked at the displays and the posters. I was secretly flattered to find that I shared my surname with Abraham Martin, one of the first inhabitants of the city, whose given name is now attached to the battlefield. Anyhow, I knew how the battle turned out from Grade 5 social studies, so we saved the fifty bucks and, packing our souvenirs, made our way back to the ferry and then back to Levis. We collected the Marmot van and bade Quebec City au revoir.

We drove along a very good stretch of the Trans-Canada highway for about an hour and pulled into a campground in Montmagny. We were touristed out, so didn't spend much time in the town, just enough to stop for some supplies (maple syrup), ask for directions, and book into what turned out to be a top-flight campground. There was plenty of space at our spot, which overlooked the majestic St. Lawrence River. The facilities were clean and generous, and the whole place was tidy and well-kept. We even had a wireless internet connection to catch up with emails.

After supper, I wandered around for a bit and was interested to see a group of people playing some sort of game on a hard-packed sand court. They welcomed me to come and watch; one of the fellows very patiently explained the game to me. I gleaned that it is called "petanque" and it is a game where you try to toss metal balls closest to a marker ball. From what I saw, it is lots of fun and a little tricky to play. I tried a toss and was surprised to find the ball quite heavy. I hung around for half an hour or so, thanked my hosts, and left the players to their fun.

Recently, I learned that in petanque, the punishment for losing a game without scoring a single point is "kissing Fanny!"

I learned that this tradition started in France's Savoy region. The first Fanny was a waitress at the Café de Grand-Lemps, just after World War I. As legend has it, she was so kind-hearted that she would allow customers who had lost a game of boules without scoring a single point to kiss her... on the cheek. This went on until one day the village mayor lost a game and came to collect his "prize." No one knows for sure if Fanny had a grudge against him and wanted to humiliate him, but we do know that she stepped up onto a chair, turned around, lifted her skirt, and offered him... her cheeks to kiss! The mayor was up to the challenge though, and less than a second later, two loud kisses resounded through the café. This was the beginning of a long-standing tradition. This is why everywhere the game of boules is played, a fake fanny is proudly displayed. The unhappy losers are obliged to kiss, in public, the generous cheeks of a Fanny, whether in a painting, a plaque made of pottery, or as a sculpture. Thus, the consolation prize has become the ultimate humiliation for boules players everywhere.

The next morning, we continued to Rivière du Loup, about an hour and a half east of Montmagny. We stayed the morning and visited two of the sights. The first was the Parc des Chutes de Rivière-du-Loup, where we had a chance to see a spectacular 100-foot-high waterfall, as well as several other smaller falls. There are footbridges to go from one side of the river to the other. One of these bridges overlooks the waterfall so we took the opportunity to pose and take a few photos. We rambled along the hiking paths and enjoyed the lookouts and "belvederes" (from two Italian words, bel, which means "beautiful" and "vedere" which means "view"), which give you an unrestricted view of the city and the river. Near the parking area there is a hydroelectric power station that is still in use, but we were not on time for a tour. Near the parking area there is a hydroelectric power station that is still in use. There was also an interesting sculpture that looks kind of like an upside down spider. Round beams of wood are hinged together to give it its overall form and a system of cables and water power provides movement so that the sculpture changes shape very slowly and continuously during the day.

Our next stop was the area near the ferry landing for the north shore of the St Lawrence. The recreational marina was something completely new to us. The boats are tied to floats and the whole shebang lies on the mud at low tide. There was a restaurant, a few shops near the ferry slip, and some nice shoreline. Being a lovely warm day, we had our lunch on a little grassy knoll overlooking the river.

Good Samaritans

It was quite a different story from my trip through the area back in 1970. I had been dropped off on the highway late in a rainy cold day. To add to the experience, I was as sick as a dog with a nasty summer cold, which I must have picked up in Montreal.

I guess I have to rewind back to Cornwall, Ontario, where I had spent the night quite happily in a community park. The day started pleasantly with sunny skies and some buns and cheese from my pack. (Buns and cheese and the occasional tin of beans had become my staple diet on the road.) I made my way to the highway and had no luck getting a ride for most of the morning. I used all the poses and antics I could think of to encourage a driver to stop. My soft shoe routine finally did the trick. I would do a couple of arm and leg cross-overs and then a hop and lean over and stick out my thumb with a big grin. It eventually worked and I had the great good fortune to get a ride with an older married couple heading back to Montreal from holiday in Ontario. Rick, the husband, introduced himself and Suzanne, and apologized that he was getting over a cold and had a bit of sniffle and cough.

I settled in the back and, as we exchanged pleasantries, I found they were very interested in my journey and said that a visit to the west coast was on their list of things to do next summer. They seemed very pleased and fascinated to have met an actual, live, starving student. As we got closer to Montreal, they offered to feed me some supper and put me up for the night, which I happily took them up on. Their place turned out to be quite a large, and by the looks of it, expensive old house.

They put me up in a bedroom that was furnished with a great big bed and dark, polished wood furniture. I took a shower and shaved in the adjoining bath and put on the cleanest clothes I had. Over a delightful barbecue supper on their patio, Suzanne told me that they had no children but they were very interested in what young people were up to and pleased to have a chance to find out what a young fellow like me thought about life. At that moment, I thought life had dealt me some pretty good cards.

I tried not to wolf down the huge steak and probably half a bushel of baked potatoes they offered me, and even tied into a green salad, which was a welcome addition to my regular diet. I was putting away a glass or two of wine as well and happily regaled my hosts with opinions on any subject they happened to raise. Eventually, I peddled them some of the adventures of my trip so far. They were a great audience and were both shocked and amused by my drug smuggling and the police chase stories.

We wrapped up the evening with a plan that Rick would give me a lift to the Trans-Canada in the morning and, full of good food and not a little drunk, I slept like a log.

Breakfast turned out to be a pretty leisurely affair and I had a chance to throw my clothes through the washer and dryer. After I got my freshly laundered things back into my pack, I sat in for a last cup of coffee and thanked Suzanne, who gave me a hug and made me think of my own mother. Then Rick and I went down to the car and off we went.

In the car, Rick was helpful, suggesting the best way to head east and suggesting some stops that I might like to make along the way as I passed through the provinces of Quebec and New Brunswick. We pulled over at the edge of the road where I planned to get out and Rick reached over and offered me his hand, saying he was pleased to have met me and I replied the same. I waved with a warm heart as I watched his car head back into Montreal.

It was after my next ride that I noticed the sniffly feeling that heralds a cold and guessed that I was coming down with something. The weather was deteriorating, so I opened my pack to get out a jacket and tucked in on the top of my stuff was a twenty-dollar bill. I knew it wasn't mine because I kept pretty close track of my money, so I guessed one of my Montreal adoptive godparents must have spotted me the cash. It really did make a big difference to me because I was getting pretty broke. I am still pleased when I think of them.

However, during the next day in La Belle Province, the sniffles and sneezes got progressively worse. The weather turned miserable to match, so by evening, when I arrived on the highway near Riviere du Loup in the rain, I was in a bit of a sorry state. I spent an hour or two sheltering beneath an underpass, but with the wet hissing back up from the pavement and the blur of oncoming traffic, it really was no wonder that no driver wanted to stop for me. Eventually, I gave it up for a bad job and crawled up the gravel slope under the overhanging concrete roadway and rolled out my damp sleeping bag.

I don't remember many other times when I was so cold, wet, sick, and lonely. The phrase "f---ed and far from home" came to my mind and I began to think about how much more travelling I wanted to do. Truck traffic thundered overhead and other vehicles hissed and snarled close below. I coughed and snorted and hawked and spat, and stared out of my fever-glazed eyes and shivered in the dark and rain.

Donna and I were having a much more lighthearted time of it these many years later. The highway to the New Brunswick border had a town called—and I am not making this up—St. Louis du Ha! Ha! We had to stop the Marmot van and take a second look at the sign. Sure enough, that's what it said. We envisioned a town of pranksters and jokesters or a school for stand-up comedians, or even a branch of the Department of Internal Revenue where they come up with new taxes, but no when we drove in it seemed pretty normal. There was an official explanation of the name, which we figured paid too much homage to history and let the opportunity for hilarity slip away.

It just didn't seem right, so we drove back to the highway and stopped for a photo shoot with Smarmy, determined to cast a little mirth on the tableau. Making goofy photos is good for the traveller's soul and soulmate.

Still pretty cheerful from our sojourn at St. Louis du Ha! Ha!, I backtracked through the photos on the camera and began to joke about one of the highlights of Riviere du Loup that I had added to our photo collection. It was the manifestation of one of the establishments often referred to as the imaginary backdrop for many risqué stories and off-colour jokes: the Motel d'Amour! There it was! For real! The owners barefacedly displayed their red and yellow neon sign for all to see right there on the street. I couldn't believe I had actually seen the Motel d'Amour!

Sadly, Donna turned down my offer to rent a room…

So Long, Quebec
Hello New Brunswick!

An hour and a half from Riviere du Loup and, according to the sign, we were "Entering New Brunswick." We made our first stop at "de la République Provincial Park." It was a delight. The park employees actually wear uniforms like in the old days. They were welcoming and made every effort to accommodate us in both French and English. They even have a deal where you get the fourth night free if you stay in provincial parks, so we got our stamp and planned to take advantage of the deal. Our campsite was great and the facilities were clean and well lit. The water was good and we even had a campfire.

New Brunswick is quite a bit like home. The forests are similar and the country has hills and valleys a lot like our Vancouver Island. It was a welcome change from the flat countryside of southern Ontario and Quebec.

The "Newbs" are great to get along with. Their most common response is "SHORE!" which has nothing to do with the edge of the sea or a lake, but roughly translates to "Sure!" As in,

"Could you fill 'er up with regular, please?"

"SHORE!"

Or "Do you have a roadmap?"

"We SHORE do!"

In no time, I was saying "shore" right along with them. Did I mention that they are bilingual? It's such a pleasant change from the chippiness about language in Quebec. In New Brunswick, there is so much more of a feeling of understanding that our ignorance of French might have something to do with the geographic fact that Nanaimo is 5,000 kilometres distant from Quebec City. That's about as far as it is from Paris to Kazakhstan.

Our first full day in New Brunswick took us to Grand Falls. We stopped in at the tourist office and asked about the river and the falls which we could see out the window. The girl pointed to the canyon in front of us and told us that during a big flood it had been full of water - right full. It was tough to imagine because it is a pretty big canyon. Later, we bought an illustrated book about the flood and, seeing the photos of the river in full force, we were amazed. Not only was the scene at Grand Falls a shock, but the aerial photo of the world's longest covered bridge at Hartland made us shake our heads as well. The water was right up to the bridge floor. All the folks we talked to as we drove through the province had stories about the flood. What impressed me was the attitude that they had come out of the flood alive and things were alright. It was quite uplifting.

We camped that night in another provincial park called Mactaquac about 15 miles west of the provincial capital. Here's its website story:

Our campground provides more than 300 comfortable and well-serviced open and wooded sites, with laundry facilities, hot showers, and kitchen shelters. The recreation centre and the mini-golf course will provide hours of fun for the kids. The camper's convenience store stocks groceries, propane, firewood, and also has a snack bar located within.

Unfortunately, it was pouring rain for us, so we missed out on the hours of fun and holed up in the Marmot van, got caught up with our diaries, and watched a recording of the British TV show "Doc Martin."

By noon the next day we were at Hopewell Rocks Provincial Park on the Bay of Fundy. We stopped in to see some pretty impressive rock formations and checked them out at both high and low tides. The tide was high when we first arrived and we viewed everything from the lookouts high above the water. We wanted to return in the morning to see the low tide scene, so we camped near Hopewell. The campground was reasonably priced, with generous well-serviced spots, although the owner and I scratched our heads and had to reboot the router to get the internet service to work. He was very helpful and told Donna and me about the history of the area. We were interested to see quite a system of dikes to create pastures to graze their animals by the sea. Evidently, the notion of dikes dates back to the Acadian settlers almost 400 years ago. We weren't clear on the present day setup. Somehow the government is obliged to maintain the dikes, although the ones we hiked around were in rough shape. There wasn't much evidence of present day agriculture that we could see.

We left the campground early and spent a magical couple of hours "Walking on the Ocean Floor" (which is a pretty catchy advert). You get access to the beach down a pretty tall set of stairs like a big fire escape. At the bottom, you step out into an amazing scene. The cliffs rise sharply so that without the fire escape stairs you cannot easily get above the water level at high tide. It is a little unnerving to think about that when you are at the bottom. You really are on the ocean floor. When the tide comes back in there will be as much as 45 feet of water above where you are standing!

Rising from the sea floor are enormous stone structures with names like Lover's Arch, Dinosaur Rock, Mother-in-Law, and ET. Best of all, because it was early in the season and quite early in the morning, Donna and I had the place to ourselves. We explored nooks and arches, and took tons of photos posing here and there among the formations.

From Hopewell Rocks, we went north to Moncton and then east to Shediac, where we took a break on our way to the Confederation Bridge. Shediac is known as "The Lobster Capital of the World" for its lobster fishing, lobster processing plants, live lobster tanks, and the famous Lobster Festival. This is where you'll find "The World's Largest Lobster!" You can even get a lobster burger.

The Bridge

It was huge! At a distance it seemed rather unimpressive, but as we drove out over the sea, it began to sink in just how big a project this was. It was also a bit scary, because most bridges have some sort of structure alongside and above as you drive across, but not this one. The closest thing to making this type of crossing is walking a railway trestle. If you have ever walked a trestle high above a river or alongside a lake, you will be able to imagine the feeling of being right up there. There is a barrier along the side, but you can easily look down over it, all the way to the ocean.

I have to wonder at the rationale for building the thing. How many people live on that Island? Actually, I am jealous. Vancouver Island is about six times bigger and has five times as many people, but we have no bridge to the mainland, just an expensive ferry system. We even joined Canada first! Probably some politicians in Ottawa have houses on P.E.I..

We drove off the bridge and decided to go to Summerside first, where we stopped for fuel. The Marmot van runs on propane and the price was $1.18 a litre, a far cry from the $0.65 a litre we paid in Alberta. We took a turn around Spinnakers' Landing marketplace, situated within a re-created fishing village, where "a potpourri of giftware, crafts, fine retail outlets, antiques, and great food await you." We strolled around, but we didn't buy much and weren't very hungry so it was back into the Marmot van for more driving. We had planned to visit some property owned by a friend, but the roads were pretty rough and we opted instead for a stop at Prince Edward Island National Park, where the sand dunes and beaches were splendid. The day was sunny and, although it was a little early in the season for a swim, it was perfect to walk along the sand in bare feet and pose smiling and waving for a photo to send back to the folks where I worked until I retired in February. Life is Good!

P.E.I. is nothing if not comfortable. The people are friendly, the water is fit to drink, and the distances are short. Even the one bum we met was well mannered! However, it is very much like a toy province—like Legoland or something. It makes you want to have your own province with a hundred thousand or so of your cousins and friends.

We decided to take a break from camping and headed for the city of Charlottetown, where we booked into a hotel. We had a pub supper and, because it was a lovely evening, ambled around for a couple hours enjoying the sights of the city before heading back to our hotel. After a day of touring the northeast of the Island, we were glad to rest up in the space and comfort of our room.

We spent the next morning in Charlottetown as well. The city is very agreeable. We ambled along a pedestrian-only area called Victoria Row visiting the various shops along the way; many specialising in handmade and locally-made items. We bought some souvenirs and then went to the farmer's market and were pleased to see lots of organic food and family producers. In the late morning we fired up the Marmot van and left the city behind.

We decided to tour the south east of the island and headed for Souris. The drive through the farmland was quite relaxing. The land is flat and the fields and farms are tidy and prosperous looking. We followed the map along straight, level roads to the seaside and across a causeway into the town.

Souris is a pretty seaside place and boasts some beautiful old buildings. We drove around a bit and decided to head back towards the causeway to Souris Beach Provincial Park for a picnic lunch. The day was warm and fine and after we ate we rolled up our pantlegs and waded along a lovely sandy beach.

The next stop was at Montague. With the tranquil river running through the town, the lovely tree-lined streets and the stately heritage homes, it really is a picturesque town. But we were drawn to the harbour to look at boats. There were some beauties there; both pleasure boats and working craft as well. It reminded us that Prince Edward Island has a long tradition of fishing as well as farming. They look pretty seaworthy and I imagine they have to be if they are to take their crews out into the North Atlantic.

From Montague, we made our way south to Wood Islands, where the ferry was to take us to Nova Scotia. We spent the night at the Wood Islands Provincial Park. The campground is situated on the shore, and we enjoyed the sea breeze along the beach in the early evening. When the wind died the mosquitoes drove us inside. We were amazed to see some other campers sitting out around their campfire. I suppose mosquito repellant is a fact of life, but we were still uncomfortable with the notion of smearing ourselves with the dreaded DEET, so we shut the screens and stayed in. Donna's cousin in Saskatchewan had told us that one of his kids had spilled some DEET on a nylon carpet and the carpet had melted.

In the morning, we drove to the ferry terminal and left the Marmot van in line while we went to investigate the lighthouse and a row of weathered replica fishermen shacks built on the other side of the small bay. Everything is built in miniature for kids, but having no kids with us, Smarmy and I had to fill in. The shacks were pretty neat and we spent a few minutes posing Smarmy in doorways and windows. We walked as far as the lighthouse and museum, it was grown-up size. Sea glass, Sea Captains, and lots of history. There was a wonderful view from the top! We still had to catch the ferry so we hustled back to the Marmot van for the hour and a quarter ride to Nova Scotia.

Nova Scotia!

The ferry took us to Caribou. We disembarked and followed the signs to Pictou, which was about a 15 minute drive. Pictou's website tells visitors:

The Town of Pictou, located on the beautiful Northumberland Shore of Nova Scotia, Canada, is renowned as the "Birthplace of New Scotland" as it was here that the first wave of Scottish immigrants landed in 1773. Here you can explore the world class Hector Heritage Quay and board the full-sized ship Hector replica. Pictou is the best place to experience old-world charm and culture and present-day hospitality.

Our visit to the ship *Hector* was very interesting. If you get a chance, it is well worth a stop not only to learn about the crossing of the settlers, but also of the restoration project itself.

The replica ship was astounding. It was obvious from the woodworking that a tremendous amount of effort and care had gone into the project. We toured both the ship and the heritage centre. The ship seemed a dangerously small vessel (only 85 foot length and 22 foot beam) to have carried its 189 passengers across the North Atlantic. It was not really a passenger ship at all.

Its cargo hold was stuffed with wooden bunks and the passengers crammed in. We were shocked at the dark and crowded conditions on board and not surprised to learn that a number of deaths had occurred during the Atlantic crossing. The bunks were stacked unbelievably tightly below decks and I imagine being cooped up in the gloom would have been nasty. There were no toilets, just a pail and no lights other than smelly fish oil lamps. Without fresh air to breathe and with nothing to do day in and day out, it must have been a dreadful and deadly voyage.

From Pictou, we headed east on the Trans-Canada to Cape Breton Island. We stopped in Antigonish for lunch. It was there that we got a few hints of another language being used: Gaelic. My mother's mother knew some Gaelic, but I had never heard her speak it and had not seen much of the language written. So seeing a sign *Ciad Mille Failte* (One Hundred Thousand Welcomes) was a new experience altogether.

We arrived at the Canso Causeway about an hour later. The causeway itself is a pretty industrial looking arrangement of power lines and railroad tracks, and rocks and gravel and transport trucks coming and going all over the place. Nothing at all like the Confederation Bridge...not as close to Ottawa I suppose.

It is still pretty impressive though, when you think that the water is a couple hundred feet deep and the base of the causeway is eight hundred feet wide down there under the water. We motored on over the Canso Strait on the swing bridge and bingo we were on the island. I like the notion that they just filled 'er up with rock so they could drive over.

There we were, on Cape Breton Island, about 6500 kilometers east from Vancouver Island. Coming off the Causeway, we saw the sign telling us the way to the

Newfoundland ferry, so away we went up the hill. We had only gone a couple of hundred yards when we saw the info centre and pulled in. The info centres in the Maritimes were a source of dismay for me. Not because they were unhelpful; no, they were quite the opposite. They spoiled my theory that info centres are mainly summer employment for someone's niece. These ones really are top notch. So we found out about some sights we'd like to see and a likely campground at Baddeck, where we planned to spend the night.

By the time we arrived at the campground, it was pouring rain so we settled into a spot. I had no adapter to plug in to the electrical service, so I went to the office to try to get one. The owner was able to provide one and we chatted a bit while he rustled up the plug for me. Small world, as they say. The campground owner spends his winters about 6 km down the road from where I live on Vancouver Island.

Next morning, we drove to Sydney with two stops in mind: the Miners' Museum and the ferry to Newfoundland. The info center was great again. But when we sat down with the ferry schedule we were sadly disappointed because the crossing to Argentia didn't begin for the season for another couple weeks. So we took the brochures and decided to go to Glace Bay and have a look at the Miner's Museum and defer a decision about the ferry 'til later.

The museum was a treat. From the moment we drove up, we were impressed. The woman at the front desk was as easy to talk to as an old friend and had a wealth of information for us. She made us feel at home right away and seemed genuinely interested in our story as well. The exhibits of mining and machinery were quite an eye-opener. My father and his brothers had mined in northern Ontario, but apart from a few old snapshots, I had no idea what it must be like to work underground.

However, I think the greatest impression from the visit was made by our tour of the miner's village. The replica company store was based on an actual store of the General Mining Association. Our interpreter was able to give us an idea of the prices and wages and the types of goods available to mining families of the period. Doing the arithmetic, it seemed impossible for the miners to get ahead. The perpetual servitude imposed on the mining community by the company store seems dreadful to me. The fact that Glace Bay's infant mortality rate was 306 per 1,000 babies at a time when the national average was 88, further points out the difficult lives of the mining families. A sad chapter of history punctuated by the mine disasters, which must have devastated many, many families.

We were in quite a solemn mood when we left the museum for Sydney. We found a park near the shore and stopped to make a bit of lunch and study the ferry brochures and talk about going to Newfoundland.

We had planned to take one ferry to the east coast of the island and then drive across and take the other ferry back, but the other ferry wasn't to start for a couple of weeks. After talking it over, we decided to save Newfoundland for the next trip. I had to admit that after nearly 8000 kilometres on the Marmot van's odometer I was ready to start back west. But before we started to reverse our direction, we took a drive to see Fort Louisburg, which turned out to be the easternmost point of our trip.

Fort Louisburg

Besides being the easternmost point we reached, it was the most interesting and engaging historical sight of our trip so far. I had heard and read about the fort, but was completely unprepared for the real thing. From the moment we were greeted by the guards in historical costume at the gate 'til we thanked them on our way out, it was like entering a time machine. The people we saw and talked to, and the buildings and artifacts made history come alive.

It was all about codfish. I had no idea what an important resource that fishery was. We learned that the military base was created for the protection of the fishery. Cod was a remarkable food. Once dried, it was cured and portable, so it could be shipped to Europe without refrigeration, which would not be available to fishermen for many, many years. The fishery, I discovered, was more important economically to France than the fur trade. Amazing! With its excellent harbour and strong fortifications, the Fortress of Louisburg became the third busiest port in that part of the world after Boston and Philadelphia.

Two and a half miles of wall surrounded the entire fort. On the western side of the fort, the walls were 30 feet high, and 36 feet across. There were two gates that led into the city. One, known as the Dauphin gate, is currently reconstructed, and the other, the Queen's gate, is not. Louisburg was also home to six bastions, two of which are reconstructed. On the eastern side of the fort, 15 guns pointed out to the harbour. The wall we were closest to was only 16 feet high and 6 feet across but it was still a substantial barrier.

Louisburg was one of the largest military garrisons in all of New France, and many battles were fought and lives lost here because of it. English and French troops fought several battles and the fortress changed hands back and forth between 1747 and 1758, when the English took the fort for the final time. The English used it to stage their attack on Quebec in 1759. After the surrender of New France in 1760, English engineers systematically destroyed the fortress and the site was abandoned within a few years.

Two hundred years later in 1961 the government of Canada undertook a project to employ out-of-work coal miners of Cape Breton in the reconstruction of about a quarter of the site. They certainly did a good job. The stone walls and buildings are amazing! It's like a portal to the eighteenth century.

We poked around in lots of buildings and talked to the people working there. We visited the cooks bustling around in a busy, noisy kitchen and stepped quietly as we admired the fortress chapel. We took a look at everything from making lace to firing muskets. The lace-makers had intricate patterns underway and how they kept track of each thread and spool was fascinating. Outside, we met one of the soldiers who was willing to pose with Smarmy and to fire her musket for us. Posing with Smarmy on her shoulder was a great shot.

The musket shot took a little longer. The first attempt was a misfire so she primed the pan again and tried again. This time it produced a loud bang and an enormous cloud of smoke erupted from the barrel that almost hid our musketeer from sight.

We also got to witness the firing of one of the fort's cannons. It was on the sea wall and the wind was feeling quite cool, so the audience was kind of huddled up close together watching the preparations and the organization of the firing crew. Suddenly the thing made a tremendous thunderclap and we did a group jolt in surprise.

Today, the entire site of the Fortress of Louisburg, including the one-quarter reconstruction, has been designated a National Historic Site of Canada and is operated by Parks Canada. I would go again in a heartbeat. It was a fantastic place.

We made our way back towards Truro, once again experiencing the joys of secondary roads. We found interesting scenery, quaint little towns, and a distinct lack of pothole fixing. By the end of the next day, we were camping near Peggy's Cove. We went to see the Cove the next morning. It was well worth it. Like the bus full of tourists that had arrived when we did, we took photos and wandered around the lighthouse and harbour. It was a picture-postcard morning and there beside the gift shop were cheerful daffodils in bloom. Springtime number six. We snapped photos and bought some postcards to take home. I do remember having an uneasy feeling as we said farewell that, although it was a beauty of a spot on a summer morning, it might be a tough place on a cold and windy winter's night.

I was reminded of the proverbial Scot, whose neighbour commented that it was a lovely summer's day, to which he replied, "Aye, 'tis a very fine morning, but I've nae doubt we'll pay for it later."

Nova Scotia is very much like home, but with lots more history. Lunenburg is not to be missed. The Fisheries Museum of the Atlantic was wonderful. We even got to take one of the replica boats for a tour around the harbour:

It was a motor boat named the *Maud R.M.* It is a replica of the original, which was an inshore fishing boat that plied its trade in the local area of Lunenburg. It was constructed on site in the Museum's Boat Shop. Each week during the summer season, a number of lucky visitors are taken for a tour of Lunenburg harbour aboard the *Maud R.M.* The tours take place each week, weather permitting. The joyful tune of the vessel's make-and-break engine fills the air!

Two of the fellas who volunteer at the museum took us down to the boat and set about getting the engine started. Now, a make-and-break engine is not just a turn-the-key-and-away-you-go kind of engine. As it was explained to me, when the great heavy wheel of the engine is given a spin by hand, the magneto **makes** electricity by means of a magnet and coils of wire. At the same time, fuel and air are sucked into the combustion chamber. The chamber is closed and the electricity sparks inside the chamber when the circuit opens or **breaks**, kind of like when you pull a plug out of the wall socket and you sometimes see a spark. Air and fuel and a spark make a fire—like a match tossed into some gas spilled on a pile of branches. Whoosh! Except that the whoosh inside the engine pushes a piston that is connected to a crank. The crank is hooked to a big heavy wheel that gets a spin. The spin starts the whole process over again and it is attached to a shaft that makes the propeller spin.

It may sound like a marvel of engineering, but in practice, quite often the person who is trying to start the engine must understand some sorcery and employ *the magic words*. The tourists are not supposed to hear *the magic words*, but very often, when the fella trying to start the engine hurts his fingers or bangs his elbow getting the heavy wheel to spin, he will mutter a few of *the magic words* under his breath before he tries again. Our guys each had a turn trying to start the engine and, sure enough, when one banged his hand, I'm pretty sure he muttered some of *the magic words*. Those words worked and the engine began its putt putt putt and we were on our way!

It was kind of foggy. As we started our tour, a foghorn was sounding from somewhere. In the fog on the water, there is a peculiar feeling of being somehow suspended in space and time. Then, when a bit of the world materializes, you're back. This happened a couple of times as bits of the shore of the bay came and went as we toured. Before long, the fog dissipated and the whole bay was revealed.

Looking back at the town, we were cheered by the brightly coloured paint on the buildings. No grey wharfside in Lunenburg! Our guides told us it was a heartwarming sight coming into the harbour from a stretch at sea. Both of them had spent their working lives fishing and told us how the fishery had declined and pointed out the fish-packing factory. Since the sale of the fishing fleet in 2003, and the decline in fish processing at the plant, the town has seen an economic decline.

Although the packaging still says "Product of Canada," it doesn't necessarily mean the fish are caught by Canadians, just that the product comes from a plant in Canada. The fish may come from the other side of the world. Going back to the dock, I learned the one more special feature of the make-and-break engine. You can slow it down, turn off the spark switch and as the big flywheel stops and then bounces backward, you give it a little encouragement, hit the switch, and presto! You get reverse as the engine runs backwards and slows down the boat.

We toured inside the museum for hours, checking out all the displays of boats and gear. After wishing I could be one of the guys working in the boatbuilding shop, we were called outdoors to take part in the launching of a model schooner. The girl running the show kindly let us put Smarmy, our mascot, aboard and the launching provided a splendid photo session. She gave me and another fella little hammers to knock out the supports and the little schooner with Smarmy aboard slid down the ways and into a tank of water. It was the first schooner launching for both Smarmy and me. I sent home a postcard with the message translated into Nova Scotian:

Well, I tot youse would like to know how we're makin' out down 'ere. Da scenery is good. Da wedder is nat so good. Cold n windy, yeah. I did git to help with de lanchin' of a schooner down Lunenburg. An I got a right nice pirate sticker for da back of da van. T'morra we're goin ta Truro ta see da tidal bore, which dey tell us is like a wee tidal wave dat comes up da rivver.

We stopped at a gas station to fuel up and, after the tank was full, asked the attendant which road to Truro was in the best shape, having discovered that some of the roads in Nova Scotia, like those we had travelled in other provinces, suffered from the dreaded pothole disease.

We proceeded indoors. I paid for the fuel and then spread my roadmap on the counter and began the interrogation of the attendant and his coveralls-wearing assistant, who got up from an old chrome chair with a half bottle of cola in one grease-stained hand and a rollie in the other. As if planning a military operation, they traced the various routes with their fingers and studied the map intently, seeking confirmation from each other about each of the possible routes. After a couple of minutes of listening to recollections as to whose cousins lived "up dat way" and where Pete's truck had broke down last month, I became a little impatient and pushed them towards actually considering which road was the better bet. I could see by the strain on their faces that they were searching hard for just the right answer to this most perplexing of quandaries. I think the sidekick had given up the struggle because he just bent his head and stared down at the map. The attendant did the same for a while then lifted his gaze and a smile lit up his face. I could see that he had solved the conundrum. His sidekick noticed, figured he was off the hook, and looked appreciatively at his colleague, awaiting the answer.

"Well-sir it really don't matter which road youse take," the attendant pronounced, "youse'll get there just the same."

A congratulatory grin blossomed on the face of his pal and looking at the happy relief on both of their countenances, I could see that I had been given the only answer I was going to get.

"Right you are," I said, and thanked them very much and hopped into the Marmot van none the wiser.

"What did he say?" asked Donna.

With a big smile, I passed on the answer: "It don't matter which road youse take, youse'll get there just the same."

On our way, we stopped in at the Ross Farm Heritage Museum located on Highway #12 in New Ross, Nova Scotia. It's just 15 minutes from the Lighthouse route, or 25 minutes from the Gloosecap trail. (It don't matter which youse take) The museum is a living, working, farm museum depicting 150 years of agriculture in Nova Scotia.

"We are a single family upland farm on land originally granted to Captain William Ross. Ross Farm Museum is still being farmed with oxen, the way it was in the late 1800s. In Rosebank Cottage, the original home of the Ross family, built in 1817, you may see food being prepared over an open fire, straw hats being woven, wool or flax being spun, butter being churned, or many other skills being demonstrated that were daily chores of the women of the time but are now almost lost."

Though it's a farm set up the way it would have been in the past, and, although I am not 150 years old, it is much like the way farms were when I was a kid. The barn had a big stone-and-earth ramp to drive up to the floor where hay and maybe other crops could be stored. Underneath were pens for livestock. Having kept some pigs from time to time, I enjoyed seeing their sow with her piglets. It's cute to hear the grunts and squeaks of the busy little guys always on the lookout for something to eat.

And the milk cows. There is something particularly calming about cows munching in a barn; it feels as if all is right with the world. I was transported back to the barn of my childhood, where there was a feeling of contentment in a dry barn on a rainy day. We never kept sheep and I know little about these animals, but one of the tourist kids declared that the Ross Farm had some nice fluffy ones and I had to agree.

The highlight of the farm tour was a bit of a walk from the barn. We walked past the lumber mill set up on the place and the path led to a small cooperage. We were delighted to visit the cooper, who had his shop near the woods. The little mill up the hill cut the wood to make the staves for the barrels. In his workshop, the cooper made the staves into buckets, tubs, and barrels. It was fascinating to see the old-time equipment, as the cooper did his magic right there in front of us. He explained as he worked how the wood was shaped, steamed, and bent, turning a pile of lumber into containers.

I was most intrigued with the straps for the tubs and pails, which were made from saplings. Evidently, somebody would choose and cut saplings about as thick as a finger for the shop while they were still green; with the bark still on, they were split lengthwise and, with the flat side in, the halves were bent around the container. A nifty cutter machine made a notch on the ends of the split bands and, magically, they slipped together and locked to hold the whole thing tight. A bucket from that shop sits beside the woodstove in our living room. We keep our kindling in it and often are reminded of that cooper.

That night we found a campground near Truro. It was an agreeable quiet evening for us and the facilities were great. After supper, I explored a little and had a chance to chat with the owner for a bit. He told me he'd had the campground for many years. It was interesting to get his take on the changing nature of campgrounds. It seems that camping is gaining in popularity and recreational vehicle owners are the majority of campers. More and more of the sites were rented year-round with the owners having a setup like a cottage ready to be used on weekends and holidays. The positive side is a reliable income for the campground owner, but it does change the nature of the place.

Next morning we were on our way home again, but before we left Truro, we went to see the tidal bore, which we were led to believe is like a tidal wave that comes up the river. That may be strictly true, but the wave is not really a frightful, towering big wall of water, it's more of an interesting, somehow misguided wave going upstream against the current rather than flowing downstream. Somehow it defies logic. We gave a wave to the tidal bore and fuelled up.

Of all the provinces we visited, Nova Scotia is my favourite. As I wrote earlier, it is very much like home, but with lots more history. It was because it was so much like home that we realized we were a bit homesick and a little travel weary. At a filling station, we talked to a fellow who noticed our license plates and remarked that he had once driven to the west coast of the country. It had taken him eight weeks to go west, but only two weeks to get home. I kind of felt the same way.

So we headed back north on Highway 104 to New Brunswick. An hour or so later, as a tribute, I stuck in a CD with Anne Murray singing "Song for the Mira" as

we passed Exit 5 to Springhill from the Trans-Canada.
I even took off my hat and placed it over my heart.

A Dip In The Atlantic

Before we leave Atlantic Canada I should include how I spectacularly dipped my hat in the ocean in 1970. If you recall I was not at all well as I hitched east from Montreal and spent one of the most miserable nights of my life shivering in the shelter of an underpass near Riviere du Loup.

The next day was not much better. Still sick and cold and wet I decided I better get someplace to dry off and try to get warm. Having misspent some time in coin laundries before, I trudged into town in search of such a facility. Luck was with me. I suppose the gas station attendant I asked for directions could see I needed a dryer and was happy to tell me there was one close by.

A coin laundry generally does not present as welcoming. I stepped inside and there were the usual washers and dryers lined up in rows and a soap dispenser stuck to a wall. Here and there were a few plastic chairs and in a cleared space a folding table with parts of newspapers strewn across it. The floors were some sort of inexpensive greyish tiles and for entertainment an there was an overstuffed bulletin board. And because it was 1970 half full ashtrays were all over the place. The smell of detergent and bleach was strong enough to make an impression even on my clogged nasal passages. It was heaven!

I wasn't home and dry but I was certainly better off than outside in the lingering drizzle. I slung my pack on the table and pulled off my damp jacket and hat. I rummaged down in my pack and dug out a somewhat dry t-shirt and pulled off the one I was wearing which was cold and damp against my shoulders and back. With a dry t-shirt on I hunted for some dry trousers. I only had two pairs so the ones out of the pack qualified as drier. Looking around I nipped in behind a row if machines kicked off my boots and did a quick change. My socks were not too bad. I emptied the pockets of my wet gear, loaded up a drier, and fed in a couple of dimes. I pulled out my towel and dried off my hair as best I could and felt a little better. The buns and cheese in my pack were in plastic so I pulled out some for breakfast. There was a coin coffee/chocolate machine near the soap machine so I got a cup of hot chocolate and sat down to a bit of breakfast. When the dryer was done the first load, I exchanged the now dry clothes for one more load of my wet stuff which included my sleeping bag. In a while all my stuff was good to go.

Good to go, but where? I needed some sleep and maybe some medicine. I found a pharmacy and bought some aspirin and a little menthol inhaler to clear my nose. Now where? I looked around and spotted a church. A church? I gave it a shot.

I entered a Catholic church and was feeling pretty lost as to what to do. I had not been in a church much for a number of years and had not been in a Catholic church more than a couple of times ever. A voice asked a question in french and its meaning didn't register for a moment as I looked around for the speaker. I spotted him and gave him a puzzled look and then declared, "I need to sleep. I am sick."

He walked over to me and put his hand on my forehead. "You have a fever" he said." Come with me."

He ushered me downstairs to the church basement and said I could sleep there. He produced a folding cot and explained that sometimes the basement was used as a shelter. There was a kitchen and he said that I should drink lots of water. I drank a glassful and took a couple of aspirin. Then I drank another glassful. He said he would check on me later on. I told him I was not a Catholic but he smiled and said "We are all God's creatures." I slept all day.

When I woke I found my benefactor had left me a sandwich and an orange. I had the orange for supper, then more water and aspirin and back to my cot. The next morning I felt ok. The fever must have passed and I was hungry. I wolfed down the sandwich. My benefactor came along and made some coffee for us.

I told him I felt much better. I told him I had little money left but asked if I could pay something. He just laughed and said the service here was free. After some talk about where I was from and where I was going I said I should be on my way. He queried if I thought I was well enough and I said yes I was certainly better. I gathered up my stuff and he packed up the cot and we went upstairs and outside. I thanked him again and said he had been a great help to me. He said, "Helping is my line of work." We shook hands and I was on my way.

The weather had cleared and it was a fine summer day as I headed for New Brunswick. I still was not one hundred percent but felt pretty chipper. I caught a ride and after an hour or so I was in Edmunston. By late afternoon I managed to get to Campbelton. I told the fella who dropped me off I wanted to see the Atlantic and he told me I was in luck because there was a nice beach and park just where he could let me off.

I got out of the car, went past the park sign, and hiked down to a lighthouse which stood there looking out over the Atlantic. Well a little of the Atlantic at least.

So this was it! Here I was. The other side of the continent! Sadly I didn't see any people to witness my amazing accomplishment. The area was set up with picnic tables and grassy areas, but nobody else seemed to be enjoying the shore. There was nothing else for it but to step down to the water and dip my hat. I put down my pack and crept up to the water till I found a spot where my feet wouldn't get too wet and ceremoniously touched my hat in the salt chuck. I pretended to pose holding up my dripping hat and then bowing this way and that for an imaginary cheering crowd. But in reality the only other person around was a girl who came walking along the shore behind me. She strolled over and asked what I was up to. I realised my performance must have made me look like a dip.

Quebec...Revisited

Quebec was easier the second time through because we now knew how to ask for camping and propane. But the night we stayed near Trois Rivières was hot and BUGGY. Little did we know that was going to set the stage for the next few nights.

The van was really hot and the screens on the little windows seemed not to be mosquito proof. You know that horrible whining sound by your face that wakes you waving your arm by your face? Then you have to hunt down the little blighter and feel even worse when you swat it only to see a big red blood smear on the ceiling or wall. That night, the walls of the interior of the van looked like an abattoir. We saw a swell T-shirt that sported a logo of a red cross with a big mosquito on it that read, "Canadian Blood Donor."

My air conditioner install turned out to be just barely adequate to cool the van after running an hour or so, so we hoped it would not get too much hotter. Truth be told, hot had not really been the rule. Cold, windy, rainy, maybe foggy, seemed to be the rule, with the odd thunderstorm thrown in for good measure. But as the temperature rose, so did the number of BUGS.

I had no idea about the variety of hateful insects intent upon dining on me. Blackflies are the most forthright. They just fly up and bite. Mosquitoes are more wily and often sneak in, hide, and wait till they hear you snore, then bite. No-see-ums shouldn't be a problem; after all, they are so tiny, but they are a problem and they do bite. I am afraid I was beginning to show signs of ISD (insect stress disorder.)

As we continued through Québec, I found myself more and more distressed by the number of insects. In the heat of the day, they would lurk in any shady spot; in the evening, it was a regular festival of bugs. I began to lose touch with reality and imagine myself somewhere in the jungles of Africa beset by the heat and the incessant torture of mosquitoes. One night Donna wakened to find me with my face beside an open sliding window breathing out through the screen. I remember reading that the carbon dioxide in mammals' breath attracts mosquitoes, so by breathing through the screen I would lure mosquitoes up to the outside. Then… BANG! SLIDE THE WINDOW SHUT AND CRUSH THE LITTLE BASTARDS! Then cackle insanely, "NYA-HA-HA-HA."

On to Ottawa...
Our Nation's Capital

Ottawa was interesting. However, it seems that parking is at a premium. I drove around downtown looking for a spot close to the parliament buildings, but all the parking was either underground or in a tower lot. Both of those options had a height restriction and the Marmot van was too tall. Then, out of the corner of my eye, I spied an underground entrance with a sign describing a 12-foot height restriction. Twelve foot height–yay!! Without a moment's hesitation, I made a sharp turn and down I went. It turned out it was a curving ramp for delivery trucks to back down at night when there was no traffic. I drove down under the building and came to a big loading dock with nowhere to turn around.

So there I was, backing the Marmot van up a curving ramp into busy traffic. Donna had to jump out and stop traffic, and even move a flustered woman who stopped right where I had to come up off the ramp and onto the street. Then she did not want to back up. At that point, Donna was not taking no for an answer..."BACK UP!"

Eventually, we found a parking spot a few blocks away. I was informed by our navigator that I now had a restriction on my driving license: no longer was I allowed to make decisions about parking places without the express permission of the navigator.

We began our sightseeing in Ottawa with a river tour because we like boats and because it was a nice calm activity after the hectic pace of city traffic. We were encouraged...

...to capture unique and spectacular views of some of the city's attractions, such as the Parliament Buildings, Canadian Museum of History (formerly Canadian Museum of Civilization), Rideau Falls, and the Prime Minister's residence. With these landmarks as your backdrop, this 75-minute cruise is the ideal way to tour the Ottawa River.

It was a swell way to learn a little history and see the sights. The tour guide was pointing out the expensive homes along the river and quoting prices like 30 million dollars.

"Why does he quote real estate prices?" I asked Donna. She said it was the oh-oh-oh response.

"The oh-oh-oh response?"

Imagine our guide as a preacher who would quote a real estate price from his guide book "This house on our left cost thirty million dollars."

And imagine us tourists as the congregation who would then give the response: "Oh-oh-oh! Thirty million!"

This peculiar adoration continued for most of the voyage.

Exploring Parliament Hill was more interesting than we were expecting, even though we didn't go inside the buildings. We had a great time admiring the architecture from the outside. There are plenty of outdoor statues to appeal to everybody. One special sight was the statue of Lester Pearson that was done by a school chum of Donna's. We had to get a photo and that little rascal of a marmot sneaked into the shot.

We stopped in at a little restaurant and got a bit of supper, then back in the van to go to the highway and find a camping place for the night. Seeing that the price of fuel was almost fifty cents a litre less in Ottawa than it had been in Québec, we fuelled up. We were to learn later that this was a special bubble of low-priced gasoline that only enveloped the nation's capital. It must be one of the perks for being in that special city. About one tankful of fuel away from Ottawa, the prices had popped back up.

An hour or so along Highway 2 heading towards North Bay, we found a very pleasant little campground on the banks of the Ottawa River. The weather had turned a bit cool, so we got ourselves set up, then we took a short stroll down to the river where we met and had a chat with the owner of the campground. When we asked about fishing in the river, she told us that, sadly, the fish in the river now were unfit to eat because of the pollution. I suppose many years of industrial waste coming into the river had taken its toll. She said fishermen still were able to catch a few and sometimes just went fishing for the fun of it and released the fish. It started to rain, so we huddled up inside the Marmot van and spent the evening catching up on our reading. The next morning we set off about 9 o'clock.

Our first stop was about an hour later at Petawawa, where we discovered that fuel was not as cheap as Ottawa. The second thing we noticed was that in and around the gas station there were a lot of people in military uniforms. I remembered that I had heard from a few soldiers that they had been stationed in Petawawa. I have recently learned that Petawawa is the largest military base in Canada. It also has quite a long history going back to 1905. During the First World War, it also served as an internment camp; during the Second World War, it was a prisoner of war camp.

From Petawawa, we kept heading toward North Bay and found a pleasant place to eat our lunch, once again looking over the river. We were quite happy to get out of the van because the highway was not a very comfortable road to drive. In my notes from the trip, I see words like spine-jarring, dishes rattling, and van bumping. So I guess it was understandable for us to be happy to take a break when we finally arrived in North Bay.

We decided to take an extended break from driving and had the van serviced with new oil and filter, went shopping for some groceries, and looked in the souvenir store, where I found my favourite T-shirt. It was a black T-shirt with a large moose on the front. The moose was wearing a Darth Vader costume and was surrounded by other forest creatures dressed in *Star Wars* regalia. The caption read, "May the forest be with you." My favourite shirt ever!

It was in North Bay where I managed to come up with a solution for a problem that had plagued us since leaving home. I had purchased the camper van a few months before we set out on our cross-country trip. When I bought it, it had low mileage and seemed to be in very good condition. The interior didn't suit us, however, so I reconfigured the accommodations and added a few upgrades. During my work on the van, I'd hardly driven it anywhere. So shortly after we left home, I discovered that it was quite unruly at highway speeds. There seemed to be some problem with the suspension in the front end. This was a real puzzle to me because I had looked at the suspension and there were new springs with the stickers still on them.

On two occasions, I had stopped in at service stations and asked for an appraisal from the mechanics; both times they reported that everything was new or in very good condition. It was in North Bay that I decided to try one last thing. It seemed to me that the tires were wearing unevenly. Perhaps those new springs were not correct. I made a guess that some extra weight in the front might compress the springs and allow the tires to sit down flat instead of slightly up on their edges. At a garden centre, I bought several bags of sand—300 pounds of it, in fact. I piled the bags up between the seats and hoped for a good effect.

It helped! For the rest of the way home, we drove with those sandbags. Back home, I discussed my solution with a spring shop and, after some investigation and measuring, found that, sure enough, the springs were the wrong ones. I had the correct springs installed and the Marmot van drove like a champ.

The cloudy and rainy weather continued, so we found a campground close to town and hunkered down for the evening. It gave us a chance to catch up with our travel diaries and consider our choice of highways for northern Ontario. Eventually, we came to conclusion that taking Highway 11 north would be the best. It gave us a chance to explore a little more of the Canadian Shield. Back in the 1930s, my grandparents had lived in a little town called Jellicoe that this highway passed through; it is where my mom and dad met and were married and we wanted to check it out.

We made an early start and I kept congratulating myself on how well the Marmot van was handling on the road. As a bonus, the road itself was an improvement over the previous day's highway. According to the information we had, we were looking at ten or eleven hours driving time to get to Thunder Bay. The Canadian Shield geography tends to become tedious enough to encourage drivers to get on with it.

Of course, we always took more than the estimated driving time. As we leisurely motored along we were constantly surrounded by lakes and rocks and forests like those we had driven through on our way east. Yes indeed, lots and lots of lakes, lots and lots of rocks, and lots and lots of forests.

Our first stop around coffee time was at Earlton, where we got fuel and had a bathroom break. We parked the van for a few minutes and stretched our legs. The sun had come out. It was a nice morning, but we had our hearts set on travelling, so we loaded up the van and were back on the highway in about 20 minutes. Fortunately, we had collected doughnuts in North Bay, and had them for a snack.

At lunch time, we pulled into Matheson and found a great little picnic spot by the lake. It was a hot day and the lake was quite nice, but there were more than a few blackflies that seemed to want to have us for lunch. The Canadian Shield has the perfect environment for all kinds of biting insects. The upside is the larvae of all those biting insects provide excellent nourishment for fish…and fishing seemed to be the main tourist attraction.

While we were driving, Donna remarked that this would be a lonely place to be stuck on the side of the road. I replied that it could be a little frightening. I began to tell her about a frightening experience I had back when I was hitchhiking through the Canadian Shield.

Barking Mad

I don't recall the exact spot on that highway which had been blasted and bulldozed out of the Canadian Shield. The roadbed wound in between lakes and rocky hillsides; sometimes the hillsides were dynamited into bits that were then hauled and dumped to fill in a small lake. There were innumerable variations on this theme. Sometimes, there were rock cuts lining one side or the other of the roadway.

I do remember there was a junction and the person I was riding with had left the main highway to travel up a secondary road. I had climbed out of the car and thanked the driver, shouldered my pack and hiked a little way from the junction. I was far enough away that I could find a good place for cars to pull over for me, but near enough that I could still get back to the junction if I wanted.

I took off my pack, set it on the ground, and took stock, finding I had enough food and water to last for a day or two. I had my trusty piece of polyethylene in case it began to rain, and enough tobacco and papers to make cigarettes to keep the bugs at bay for at least a day. I proceeded to roll up a cigarette because the bugs had already discovered my whereabouts.

I suppose it was the smell of the burning tobacco that gave away my position. There was a rock cut behind me that created a short wall probably about 5 or 6 feet high. I never expected anyone to be on top of that wall, let alone a raving maniac.

Not that I'm any kind of expert on madness, I certainly had very little experience with any sort of lunatic up to that point in my life. I had read about characters who were "barking mad" and, in conversation, had heard about guys who were "as crazy as a shithouse rat," but I had never spent much time in the company of the dangerously insane.

So I was completely unprepared when an old man sprang up from the top of the rock wall and announced that he was a lizard. My eyes travelled up the plaid shirt to the long grey hair that lay in oily coils on his shoulders. His gaunt and wrinkled face looked down toward me. His eyebrows were the kind that grew bushy and wild, making an overhang to shade his eyes. His eyes were dark and gleamed menacingly from their deep recesses. And they were checking on me every minute. He reminded me of a newscaster who steadily faces his audience. Perhaps it was more like a vulture or a snake watching its prey. Anyway, it was pretty unnerving the way he concentrated on me. He didn't say another word for quite a while.

At first I thought I might've misheard or misunderstood; then he spoke again repeating that he was a lizard. He went on to say that he liked to lie in the sun and he did not like tobacco smoke. He told me he had been living on that rock for a thousand years. I put out my cigarette, picked up my pack, and headed back to the junction. I had hoped that if I kept a safe distance between us, I might come out of this all right. I had no idea what a safe distance might be but figured at least I could have a head start and could probably outrun him for a period of time. He didn't seem to try to come down off the top of the rock   wall but he had not finished with me.

"This is my rock!" He yelled. "You can't have it! Don't try to sneak up on me! I know ten ways to kill you!"

I picked up my pace, all the while glancing back like a dog on a leash to see what he was up to, and then glancing around searching for a likely rock or chunk of wood that I might use if he attacked me. He continued his tirade and I kept going until I got back to the junction. I was kind of stuck and didn't know what to do next, but figured at least now I had two escape routes.

I had turned completely around and was watching him. He'd stopped yelling, but I could still hear him muttering to himself. I did not want to enter into any kind of interaction with the lizard man, but I could not see a quick way out of the situation. By now I was convinced that I should keep a couple of big rocks handy because he looked pretty unstable. I also figured that I should keep an eye on him as much as possible. That part at least wasn't difficult. He had stretched out on the top of his rock with his head and shoulders near the edge so he could watch me.

Luck was with me because a pickup truck came along the side road. His turn signal told me he was going my way. The driver faced me through the open passenger window and asked me if I wanted a lift to Thunder Bay.

"Oh yes, please," I answered. I tossed my pack in the back and jumped into the cab, and off we went. Evidently he didn't see lizard man watching us and I didn't point him out.

Our present day journey through northern Ontario was not nearly so eventful, just lots and lots of miles and miles of rocks and trees and lakes and bugs. We made a point of stopping at Jellicoe because there was a bit of family history. We fuelled up at the Jellicoe general store and took a little drive around.

There was one other point of interest that we wanted to see before Thunder Bay because we had read about an amethyst mine that we might visit. But when we found out that the road was pretty rough and steep from the highway to the mine, we decided against a detour. It all turned out for the best because Lo! and Behold! we found a gift shop near the highway that had all kinds of amethyst. We spent half an hour happily nosing around and came away with some raw chunks of amethyst and a couple of pieces that had been crafted. We have one little piece that looks like a small tree on a knoll that sits in the window by our kitchen table.

HOORAY! We came up with a solution for the bug problem!

Step 1: check into hotel

Step 2: get screens for front windows

Step 3: get out of Ontario

We spent the night in a hotel in Thunder Bay and managed to feel much better about the trip. We had a respite from the bugs and were able to move around without bumping into each other. You don't realize what a luxury space is until you spend a month or two living in a camper van. It was a great idea and we both congratulated ourselves on taking a break for a little rest and relaxation.

On our way again the next day, we realized why Thunder Bay had such an appropriate name. What thunderstorms! And rain! It was like someone repeatedly throwing pails of water against the windshield. Thunder Lake and Thunder River and two days of storms. To top it off, we had a close encounter of the moose kind.

We had stopped for a fill up of gas a day or two earlier and noticed a vehicle with a lot of damage. When I quizzed the gas station attendant, he said that the people driving it were okay and that they'd had a close encounter with a moose. He went on to tell me that a lot of people end up hitting a moose because moose will rush out of the bush and run straight across the highway. To make things doubly difficult, a cow moose will very often run across to be followed shortly after by a calf. The gas station attendant told us that a lot of accidents happen because people hit the second moose.

I had glimpsed up from the road to look in the rear view mirror because a minivan came speeding up behind me and was tailgating waiting for a place to pass. It was absolutely shocking when a great big moose jumped out of the bush and ran across in front of us. I braked hard and ended up stopping on the shoulder just before I would have hit the moose—close call! The minivan behind nearly hit us and was never going to stop in time, so the driver swerved around us and just missed the second moose by a whisker. Fortunately, everybody survived the encounter, but I kept a sharp eye out for the double moose trouble after that.

Prairie Vikings

After we escaped from Ontario, we decided to seek further amusement by visiting Gimli, Manitoba. What an unlooked-for delight! We had already visited Winnipeg and I remembered reading about Gimli's ties to Iceland, and by extension to Vikings. Donna agreed that it would be a glimpse at an interesting bit of Canadian history, so we left Highway 1 at the Whiteshell Provincial Park turnoff onto Highway 44 and then made a small detour to the West Hawk Lake Campground. It was a very nice overnight spot, where we had stayed on our way east. One couldn't ask for a prettier campground. After our supper, we hiked to the lakeshore and enjoyed the sunset and then made out way back to our campsite in the fading light.

The next day we followed Highway 44 northwest to Highway 9 and a quick stop in Selkirk for fuel and snacks. That same highway took us north along the southwestern shore of Lake Winnipeg to Gimli.

Arriving on a hot Sunday afternoon, we walked around the docks at the marina and stopped to talk to a sailor, who turned out to be from Sidney, Nova Scotia. Bob (the sailor) told us that the fish of choice was pickerel and a good dinner could be had in any of several eateries on the main street. Donna chose pan-fried and I had deep-fried and, you know, pickerel are very good eating.

We camped that night near town and went back in the morning to see the museum. We were killing time before it opened, so we stopped and talked to some fishermen who were bringing in their catch. They go out in fairly small boats—mostly one or two guys. We also found out that although the lake is the tenth largest lake in the world, incredibly it is only 30-odd feet deep for the most part. They fish with nets; they even ice-fish in winter. Pretty neat how they string the nets under the ice in the winter: employing trained beavers…wink, wink, nudge, nudge. Then we visited the Icelandic Museum, which told how the newcomers from Iceland had come to found a colony on the west shore of Lake Winnipeg. They arrived in 1875. Called "New Iceland," the colony was one of the earliest group settlements in the West. Today, the reserve of land originally homesteaded by the Icelandic pioneers is part of Manitoba's Interlake region. We enjoyed the displays showing pioneer life. The re-creation of an early house and the boats and fishing gear displays were fascinating. The museum also had an additional display about Vikings. I got to horse around with the swords and axes when the curators weren't looking. Turns out, Vikings lived in Norway, Scotland, Ireland, and parts of England, among other places. Turns out all my grandparents came from Norway, Scotland, Ireland, and parts of England. I am spelling my name RALF from now on.

We had a great photo opportunity with their giant Viking statue, and we learned about *Islendingadagurinn*: the Icelandic Festival of Manitoba. *Islendingadagurinn*, as far as we have been able to determine, is the second oldest continuous non-indigenous ethnic festival in North America. The first Icelandic festival in North America was held in Milwaukee in 1874. The first Icelandic Festival in

Manitoba was held in Winnipeg in 1890, was held there annually until 1931, and since 1932, has been held in Gimli.

The festival was still a number of weeks in the future, so we contented ourselves with *Islendingadagurinn* hats to take home. Donna bought some fresh pickerel and we headed homeward.

We headed back south towards Winnipeg, but decided to give Winnipeg a pass on the way home, so we took secondary highways to go north of Winnipeg but staying south of Lake Manitoba, eventually getting onto Highway 16, the Yellowhead. As was often the case on our trip, we found that some of the secondary roads were pretty rough. And with all the rain, the potholes were filled with water, which made them a double hazard because not only are they hard on the vehicle's suspension, but the water disguises how deep they might actually be.

I am reminded of a story about former Prime Minister, Pierre Trudeau. With an election coming up, the Liberals were looking for ways to get the name of their candidate in front of the voting public. They came up with a magnificent idea. The plan was to create signs–bilingual of course–for the entire length of the Trans-Canada Highway, with the intention of marking all the water-filled potholes on the road. The beauty of the plan was that in French, a water filled pothole could be translated as a "trou d'eau."

The prairies have really BIG sky. It is fascinating. It's almost hypnotic if you are driving on really straight roads and especially neat if you want to stop and daydream looking for shapes in the clouds. If I lived on the plains, I would have to spend a lot of my time lying on the ground watching the clouds and turning my imagination loose to wander wherever. However, that's not such a good idea when you're driving on roads that resemble a World War One battlefield. It can get tiring, but you must remain vigilant or end up having your car repaired. We drove as far as Neepawa, by which time we were really ready to get out of the Marmot van.

On the east side of town, just off Highway 16, is the Lions Riverbend campground. It is advertised on the town's website:

Lions Riverbend Campground is located just off Highway #16, at 500 Broadway Avenue. The campground is open from May to September each year and has sites for all types of RVs. There are over 70 sites available with sewage disposal, washrooms, drinking water, and showers located in the immediate vicinity.

The campground is located right beside the outdoor swimming pool (offering complete Red Cross swimming lessons). Also close by are the 18-hole golf course, walking trails, fishing, picnic areas, and baseball diamond. The campground site is only a short distance from Neepawa's downtown shopping centre.

All of this and at a reasonable price! Good old friendly Manitoba! Ever since our stay in Russell on our eastward trek a number of weeks earlier, I had a warm feeling about Manitoba. Neepawa did not disappoint. The campground was great and the town lived up to its billing as the most beautiful town in Manitoba. Author Margaret Laurence wrote several books through the 1960s and 1970s depicting the town under the name of Manawaka. The next morning, we continued on Highway 16 to Minnedosa, where we had stopped on our eastward journey. Although we had enjoyed our previous visit, this time we decided to carry on and, because there was a junction with Highway 10 to Brandon, we made a left turn and headed for Highway 1.

Evil Clowns

As we left Brandon on Highway 1, we passed a spot that I recognized because I had spent a day and a half there when I was hitchhiking all those years earlier. Then, as now, I had been on my way home. I had spent a couple of days in Winnipeg, which was a lot of fun.

One of the things that sticks in my memory was a giant cake for the centennial. The province of Manitoba was created in the summer of 1870 and to mark 100 years the summer of 1970 was one of celebrations. With everyone from Queen Elizabeth II to Janis Joplin participating it was a great place to be. To mark the occasion, Winnipeg had an enormous cake on the grounds of the legislature. There was a guard on a chair at the base of the cake with a pretend shotgun, which was chained to the chair as I recall. It had been a point of speculation whether or not we could steal the gun for a souvenir. Ahh, kids...

Unfortunately, I had spent pretty much all of my money including some cash that I had earned working on a farm in Ontario. So there I was on the side of the road near Brandon hoping for a ride and feeling a little frustrated because no ride had been forthcoming. This was beginning to feel a lot like Wawa.

In early afternoon, which would've been after lunch, if I'd had any lunch, I decided to walk back into town. I passed a few other hitchhikers and one of them explained to me that this was a pretty tough place to get a ride because there was a story circulating that a local priest had recently been killed by a hitchhiker. That did explain the reticence of drivers to offer a ride.

By the time I got into town, I decided to wire home for a bit of cash. I had left a few dollars in my bank account for just such an occurrence. It was getting late in the afternoon by the time I began the arrangements and was told that my money should be ready the next morning. It was Friday afternoon.

I rummaged through my pack hoping to find something to eat but no luck. I thought perhaps I might get a bit of food if I approached a restaurant and offered to do a little work. You know, wash dishes for a meal or something like that. All I managed was to get a glass of water.

In those days, there was quite a fellowship of travellers, most of whom could be recognized quite easily by the packs they carried. It wasn't long before I managed to meet a couple of my fellow travellers and asked where there was a good place in town to camp overnight. They told me that they had spent last night in a great park by the river. They were heading there themselves and I was welcome to go along with them. I learned that they were coming from Ontario and were planning to go to Vancouver. They introduced themselves as Gary and Linda, and I introduced myself as well. They said they had been trying to catch a ride out of town for too long and had given up. They were taking the bus tomorrow.

The bus! What a great idea. We hiked to the park and headed for the place where they had camped the previous night. It was a great spot. It was out of the way and covered by a big tree in case of rain. They were well equipped and had groceries with them and invited me to share a meal. I explained that I really didn't have much to contribute but they said that was no problem. After we ate, we consulted the bus schedule they had picked up and I explained that I was collecting some cash in the morning. The 11 o'clock bus looked perfect.

The office opened at 10:00, so I could nip in and get the cash, grab a couple of eats, and be on the 11:00 bus. Well, I could have if it wasn't for the evil clowns. I hate clowns.

The Manitoba Act was proclaimed on July 15, 1870, when Manitoba entered into Confederation and became Canada's fifth province. Saturday morning was a big celebration in Brandon. like everywhere else in Manitoba, they were having a 100th birthday party that July day.

When I left the park, I was completely unaware of the scope of the festivities, but soon found myself part of a crowd on the parade route. It turned out to be problematic when I realized that the office where I was to collect my cash was on one side of the parade route and the bus depot was on the other side a few blocks over. I was on the same side as the bus depot, so I had to cross twice to get the money and get the bus and the parade was already underway.

So I stood and watched as a couple of the parade participants marched past and decided that it shouldn't be too difficult to casually slip across the street in the space between some of the celebrants.

It was made even easier when one of the floats gave me the perfect opportunity. The people on the float were tossing candies to the children along the route. So lots of children and a few adults were darting out into the street to collect the goodies. It wasn't too difficult for me to dart out on one side and slip across to the other side before the next group of marching participants came along. So far so good.

It was only a matter of minutes and I was into the office, did the paperwork, and had a bit of cash in my pocket. I eased my way through the crowd up to the street and was preparing to make another dash across and be on my way. And it would've worked out fine if it hadn't been for the clowns. Did I mention that I hate clowns? Let me tell you why.

These clowns were on bicycles. There was a pack of them. They were slipping along the edge of the parade like wolves just waiting for one of the herd to drop out. Clowns are opportunists. They test their prey, sensing any weakness or vulnerability. Clowns are ambush predators that rely on the element of surprise and a short and intense burst of energy to secure their prey. They spot their prey, and single one out to make fun of them. When I stepped out into the street, I was quickly surrounded. There was a great deal of hilarity as the clowns had me surrounded. Each time I tried to politely slip across the street, they blocked my way. They honked their horns and made their exaggerated gestures like traffic cops and blew their whistles, much to the delight of the crowd. I was not so delighted. In fact, I really wasn't enjoying the performance at all. They would not listen to my polite requests to get across the street. I didn't really see a way out of it other than going back where I had come from but they wouldn't let me do that either and I began to feel a little panicky. The more I was discomfitted, the happier the clowns and the crowd were.

But then, in a flash of inspiration, I remembered a lesson I had learned from my high school PE teacher. It really wasn't part of the curriculum, but it was a lesson that had proved very useful for this particular situation. My PE teacher had been a city policeman in England before he had come to Canada. One day he was telling us about having to deal with an unruly gang. He and his fellow coppers would have been very happy to have packed off one or two of the ringleaders to jail, but they really had no visible reason for doing so. However, if one of the gang members had accosted one of the police, they would have had ample reason to haul them off. It was then that he explained to us that if you have a good pair of boots and you tread, unnoticed, down the ankle of someone, it is quite painful. If you do that while being face-to-face with a gang member, the odds are they will react violently and then you have free reign to whack them a couple of times and haul them away.

Well, I had a good pair of boots on. I found that a pair of solid work boots with thick leather soles was a great asset for life on the road. Putting into practice that wonderful lesson from my high school teacher, I found myself very close to the ankle of one of the clowns who had parked right in front of me with his near foot resting on the pavement and his away foot on the pedal of his bicycle. Unnoticed, my boot grated down his ankle causing him to yelp and try to jump away. Being on a bicycle, jumping away was difficult, but tipping over on the bicycle and crashing to the asphalt was easy. The crowd loved it. With one clown down and the others coming to help him up, the focus had shifted away from me and I managed to back out of the situation and ease away to the sidewalk that I wanted. As I glanced back, I saw that my victim was explaining to his pals what had happened and the faces of the malevolent clowns were now searching the crowd for me. One of them spotted me and I smiled and saluted him as I left them to their fun. The old one finger salute!

It was a few blocks to the bus depot and by the time I got there I had just enough time to purchase my ticket, and grab a snack. I stowed my pack in the luggage area underneath and climbed aboard the bus. Adios Brandon. Adios clowns!

The Twilight Zone

By the time I had finished my reminiscence of fun times in Brandon, we were back on the Trans-Canada heading west. Driving on prairie highways again was not particularly exciting. The highway just goes straight to the horizon which keeps receding like the end of the rainbow We were usually able to see when storms were approaching so we were very surprised when suddenly it was darker and the rain began.

Early in our journey, our camping guide said that we might find convenient camping at municipal parks in small towns in many places in Canada. So far, that had proven to be true. So in the middle of a thunderstorm in Saskatchewan, we pulled off the highway into a small town. We soon saw a sign that directed us to their park. The thunder and lightning and the heavy rain had forced us off the highway and, unbeknownst to us, forced us to cross over into ***the Twilight Zone.***

We were relieved to find the park because we were quite ready to stop driving for the day. There wasn't really much to recommend the place though, other than the fact that you could stop there and they had washrooms. It was pretty much a small field with a lane that went up one side, circled around at the end and went down the other side, with a few feeble trees here and there. Through the rain-streaked windshield,

I read the sign near the entrance with the usual proclamation welcoming campers, the camp regulations, and advising that campers might choose to put their camping fees into an envelope and deposit it in the drop box once they had chosen a site that they liked. I decided to jump out of the van and make a run for it to the dropbox to collect an envelope and, when the rain had passed, come back and drop my fee into the dropbox. However, the envelopes were kept in a container that was cleverly made so that the lid was stiff enough to stay open during rainstorms. The envelopes were a sodden mess. Not wanting to spend any more time in the rain than necessary, I decided to deal with the fees later.

We eased along to choose a site, which was pretty easy to do because the place was almost deserted. There was only a rundown trailer in a corner of the park. It looked as if someone was living there full time; perhaps an itinerant worker who moved his trailer from job to job. Evidently the owner had quite a taste for beer because there was a rather large pile of empties underneath the small awning with duct tape patches attached to the side of the trailer. There were a few other odds and ends, including a spare wheel, a rickety looking barbecue, and a few jumbled storage tubs.

Not wanting to crowd the only other occupant of the park, we drove partway around the circular lane and wheeled into a spot that seemed level enough and parked. While we waited for the rain to ease off and the sky to lighten a bit, we had a cup of tea and a cookie and settled in to do a little reading. The park was surrounded by the residential streets of the town.

I had a peculiar feeling of being watched and when I looked up from my book I could see through the gloom a woman with grey hair staring out from what appeared to be her kitchen window. Because of the privacy film on the van windows, she could not see me. Still, it was a little bit unnerving. It got even more weird when she slipped out of her back door and entered the park through a gate at the back of her property. She glanced furtively from under the hood of her coat spying on our vehicle as she slinked across the far side of the park. She appeared to be going to the building that housed the washrooms and that had the camping fee envelopes and dropbox fixed to the outside wall. I suppose she must have checked the fees box while she carried out her surveillance. A moment later, she scurried back to her house, checking on us like a weasel watching a henhouse all the while.

I mentioned to Donna that we were the objects of quite a bit of interest from the old lady living beside the park. Donna speculated that by the looks of things, probably not much happened around here and so we were probably a bit of a novelty. I went back to my book, but I wondered about the vigil-aunty eyeing us and inspecting the fee box. It's now my belief that she was an informer because soon after she returned to her surveillance post we were visited by the park warden. The warden was not wearing a Gestapo uniform, but it really would have suited her. She raced in to the campground and parked on the other side of the lane from our spot. Quickly she strode across in the rain and pounded on our side door.

Donna opened the door and was greeted by, "You did not pay the camping fee. Didn't you read the sign?"

I joined Donna at the door and explained that when I had checked the envelope container I couldn't find a suitable envelope. I further explained that the combination of paper, glue, and water was excellent for making a papier-mâché object—perhaps a snowball or a miniature iceberg—but the envelopes were quite unsuitable for the intended purpose of collecting fees for the dropbox. Then I asked to be reminded how much the fee would be.

"You will have to pay for two nights because you were observed staying here last night and did not pay the fee." she accused.

I explained that there must be some mistake because we were in Manitoba last night. Donna went to fetch the receipt from the Neepawa campground.

"Oh yes, that old story. *We were somewhere else.* This brown van was seen here last night and seen leaving early in the morning without paying."

Donna handed her the receipt that contained the name of the Neepawa campground, which was dated the day before.

"This could be a made up receipt," the warden snapped, as she studied it as if it might have been a forgery. Eventually she shoved the rain spattered paper back at Donna.

"Well, I still have to collect the fee due for today so there is no chance of you sneaking out without paying."

Donna said that we would not be sneaking out at all; rather, we would be leaving immediately. I took the hint and slipped into the driver's seat. As I fired up the engine, I couldn't quite hear what Donna said next, but I believe it had something to do with where the warden could shove her fees and her wet envelopes.

As I drove around the circular lane, I glanced up and there was the vigil-aunty staring at us from her surveillance post. I imagined I could hear Rod Serling's voice as we made our way out of the park and back onto the highway:

"And so our hapless travellers caught in a thunderstorm have unwittingly made a detour through

The Twilight Zone."

Indian Heads and Moose Jaws

After escaping from the Twilight Zone, we found ourselves back on the highway with the storm behind us and a nice sunny late-afternoon drive ahead. However, even though I had a desire to put some miles between us and the aptly named town of Dreadfull, I didn't really feel like driving for hours and hours. Happily, I noticed a road sign announcing exits to Indian Head coming up.

I told Donna that I had camped there with my mother and brother back on my very first cross-country expedition and that it was a swell place for a stop. We pulled off the highway, followed the signs, and came to the Indian Head campground. It was lovely. The sun was shining on the flowers planted around the office, which was a cozy little log cabin building, and the camp operators could not have been more pleasant and obliging. We signed in and I explained that I had camped here with my family in 1966. I joked that I was a returning customer, which brought a smile to the face of the owner.

After supper, we looked around and cruised the town a bit. We had to stop for a good look at the big Indian Head. The statue was built in 1985, and was a total height of 18 feet. It weighs 3,500 pounds and is constructed of metal pipe, metal mesh, and three coats of cement. The statue has appeared in numerous television commercials and is located in the southwest corner of the town of Indian Head on the north side of the Trans-Canada.

I found it interesting to learn how the town got its name. There are several versions of how it came to be called Indian Head. Some are more believable than others.

One version that sounds plausible comes from information at the Indian Head Museum and from Chief Albert Eashappie's account recorded in the Indian Head and District history book.

Many First Nations people were stricken by diseases like smallpox, which were introduced by fur traders who traveled through this area. Local First Nations people used the hills south of the current town site as their burial grounds, but many bodies were not buried at all, so great was the fear of contracting the disease.

Over the years, the First Nations people came to call the burial ground the Many Skeletons Hills or Many Skulls Hills. The new settlers who came to the area referred to them as the Indian Head Hills.

When the Canadian Pacific Railway laid track through this area in 1882, the new settlement where the railway station was built needed a name. The townspeople wanted the name Indian Head Hills, and offered the First Nations people a camping ground near the town in exchange for the name.

The town became Indian Head, without "Hills" perhaps because it sits on a fertile, relatively flat, plain.

Early the next morning, we were again on our way across that plain. Our first stop in was Moose

Jaw. It was a fine morning and a wonderful opportunity to visit Mac the Giant Moose. Yes, a giant moose in Moose Jaw is pretty much what the average traveller would expect. But completely unexpected is a glimpse into Moose Jaw's history. Who would have thought that you might get a chance to experience the story of early Chinese immigrants to Canada and to check out what it might have been like in the era of gangsters and rum runners.

The Tunnels of Moose Jaw is a year-round attraction and provides guests with some unusual history and excitement. Moose Javians have told stories of the tunnels under the city for decades. Boys, now men, played in them as children, much to their parents' dismay.

Residents' stories of being led blindfolded through underground spaces have been repeated at dinner tables for years. Their purposes have been argued and disputed with many an old-timer claiming to have the real scoop. Over the years, merchants have blocked up many of these spaces. Others, under downtown hotels, have been filled in following fires or demolition. Only a few are known to remain.

The stories of tunnels under Moose Jaw come alive in two interactive theatrical tours. Guests become part of the underground experience, travelling beneath the streets of Moose Jaw. History has never been more exciting. You can walk by the site of the early Chinese immigrant, and then lie low with the infamous Al "Scarface"Capone. Yes, Moose Jaw was a centre of bootlegging, prostitution, gambling, and corruption. We did not indulge in any of the aforementioned vices. We heeded the call to Alberta and the Dinosaur Museum at Drumheller, so we left that den of iniquity behind and were back on that long prairie highway again.

Dinosaurs! And Bunnies?

Drumheller was even better than expected, and we had already been thinking it might be pretty good. Actually, Drumheller was rather unexpected. There we were, driving from the south on a secondary highway across the prairie, and shazam! The road plunged into an incredible valley. The sides are all layered in different textures and colours and have a science fiction look about them. The bottom of the valley spread out before us with a view of the river and lots of homes and businesses. It is quite a surprising find; a hidden settlement.

Our first stop was the info centre. Wonder of wonders, here was an info centre that was chock-full of helpful people and good information and was, in fact, open when we wanted to visit. We were able to plan our visit, get tips on the local sights and accommodations from knowledgeable staff, and suitably armed, were quite excited to head for the giant, (really, really, big) dinosaur.

Their dinosaur is 86 feet tall! That is 4½ times the size of an actual *Tyrannosaurus rex*. The kid in me really got excited. Donna was not quite that excited, so she stayed on the ground to take photos of Smarmy and me at the top. We climbed to the top of the stairs with all the kids and found ourselves at the lookout, which is actually built inside the dinosaur's gaping mouth. She got some great pictures, and Smarmy and I got a view of the valley. Next we went into the obligatory gift shop and then down the street with Smarmy playing with the dinosaur statues that were all over the place. Next we were off to the Royal Tyrrell Museum. What a wakeup call for the old brain!

The museum is huge. There are all sorts of displays of skeletons and dioramas with full-size dinosaurs complete with prehistoric sounds. (I think two college kids with a mike and a sound system were "arrrging" in the background.) All the geological ages are described with way too many names for me to manage. I was enthralled with the sea creatures that looked like Star Wars extras. The sea creature display is dark. You stand on a glass floor with some creatures below, some in front, and some above and, as the narration goes from one example to the other, the corresponding critter is spotlighted. Very well done. I also liked the "Plasticene" Period mammals with big fangs. I used to delight in making plasticene animals myself when I was a kid.

"Dinosaur Hall", has over 40 mounted dinosaur skeletons, including specimens of Tyrannosaurus rex, Albertosaurus, Stegosaurus and Triceratops. "Lords of the Land" is a display of fierce raptors perched atop pedestals and dramatic death poses. These creatures are nature's very own works of art. "Age of Mammals" and "Ice Ages" cover mammalian life from the first tiny critters to a magnificent Mastodon and Sabre-tooth tiger. The creatures of the seas are well represented, but the most spectacular is the "Triassic Giant", a 1,700 square feet (160 m2) fossil specimen of the world's largest known marine reptile, the 21 metres (69ft) long Ichthyosaur.

We spent most of the day at the museum and finished up with a look around outside, which had some interesting landscapes and some outdoor dinosaurs. But all good things come to an end and we decided we needed to find a campground for the night.

We camped in the valley in a great campground by the river. After we got set up, we realized we were surrounded by bunnies - tons of the little rascals! The campground lady had several bunny pens, but it looked like most of the inmates were out on day passes. We had a bit of a laugh as we watched a couple of little kids in a neighbouring site chase bunnies for a while. The bunnies didn't seem too worried and kept just out of reach of their pursuers. It kept the kids out of their parents' hair for a bit and provided Donna and me with a little entertainment while we sat on out camp chairs. What could be cuter than a toddler and a bunny?

The day had been quite a warm one. The late afternoon was pleasant and cooler as we busied ourselves making supper, doing the washing up and building a campfire. We enjoyed the evening just sitting by the campfire and talking about the next day's destination - the Rockies.

The Rockies

Before we called it a night, we took a little time for some route planning. We had thought to go south to Waterton Lakes National Park, but the temptation to zip over to Banff was too much. Because I had no desire to drive through Calgary, we took a secondary highway cross-country through Airdrie and Cochrane. We didn't realize how much we had missed the mountains until we began to see them in the west.

We joined the Trans-Canada near Morley. We had not travelled very far when we found a bear jam. I was unfamiliar with bear jams, not having seen one before. For those of you readers who have not been to a bear jam either, I must tell you it is a traffic jam with bears. You create one by spilling a boxcar full of grain beside a highway in the mountains. Bears soon come for free food. Lots and lots of bears. They pig out and have a frolic. Then tourists stop their vehicles to see the bears and take photos. In their excitement, the tourists seldom make a very good job of parking their vehicles well out of the path of traffic. The traffic, of course, contains more tourists who are slowed down by the badly parked vehicles, notice the wildlife, and get excited and park badly themselves. And so it goes. Hopefully, the tourists don't get too close to the bears, as in the old poem:

Algey met a bear.

A bear met Algey.

The bear was bulgy.

The bulge was Algey.

Eventually, we made it through the bear jam and were able to enjoy the mountain scenery without so much traffic and confusion to worry about. Every time I travel through the mountains, I feel what has been described as a mountain high. The vistas literally lift my vision to lofty heights and lift my thoughts at the same time. The size and majesty of mountains overwhelm day to day details and wash away cares. Imagination is allowed to climb where it will. There is something refreshing and exciting about entering mountain passes. By the time Donna and I rolled into Canmore we were infected with the excitement of the peaks. We were like two squirrels chattering about what we wanted to see and do.

We arrived in Canmore about noon. The townsite was originally a stop on the transcontinental railway. It was named Canmore in 1884 by Donald A. Smith, a Canadian Pacific Railway pioneer. By the late 1800s, the area was booming because of the abundance of coal. Several mines were worked and abandoned. For more than a half century, the Canmore mines and the small community continued on, braving ownership changes, fluctuating coal markets, and increasing protests from conservationists. In 1965, Canmore was incorporated as a town with 2,000 residents. By the 1970s, Canmore's coal industry was suffering. On July 13, 1979, it was all over. Canmore Mines Ltd. ceased coal production and 120 miners were out of work. It was the end of an era.

In the early 1980s, the mountain village would be the site of Nordic events for the 1988 Winter Olympics, an event that breathed new economic life into the beleaguered community.

Since the Olympics, Canmore has more than quadrupled its population of 3,000 to almost 14,000 citizens. Now, instead of a beleaguered coal mining town, it is one of the most sought after recreational and residential areas in Alberta. I have visited Canmore a number of times and see no reason to call the residents Canmorons despite the famous Royal Canadian Air farce character "Mike from Canmore".

I hunted some residential streets 'til I found what I was looking for: a cabin that held some special memories. I knocked, but no one was home, so we took a couple photos of the old place and decided to drive across town to visit some friends. They had a big new house right on the river. It was a beautiful warm day and we had a lovely afternoon of visiting sitting on their deck overlooking the Bow River with a backdrop of the Rocky Mountains. Canmore is truly a beautiful place.

I had first visited Canmore and seen the little cabin on my hitchhiking trip. From Brandon, I had taken the bus to Calgary. I arrived in Cowtown in the morning and didn't hang around very long because I was anxious to be on my way home. It took quite a while to reach the outskirts of the city, but by noon I was at the highway. Fortunately, I caught a ride with a woman and her adult son who were heading to Lake Louise. They were very personable and asked me about my travels and I kept them entertained with a few of my exploits. They had coffee in a big thermos and provided me with a cup and a couple of donuts.

For some reason, I decided to stop in Banff, so I asked to be let out at the turnoff into the town. They told me they would let me out at the western turnoff, which was much closer to the townsite than the eastern one. I thanked them, both for the ride and the pleasant company, grabbed my pack, and waved as they sped on up the highway. I hiked into town and found myself one of many young travellers. Some had Banff as a summer destination, and many found it a great place to stop over whether they were heading east or west. I had a bit of lunch at a café and got some cheese and buns for my pack, and hung around and visited for a while. I learned that rides were hard to come by; not as bad as at Wawa, but not great. I figured to try for a ride for a while and maybe spend the night in Banff if my bad luck from Brandon continued.

I was thinking about the remaining miles to get home while I was walking back towards the highway. Somehow things did not seem to be going my way. While I was reflecting on the events since of the past few days, I had stopped by the side of the road to roll up a smoke, when something quite unexpected happened.

Being well used to appraising the driver and occupants of passing cars and estimating the chances of catching a ride, I usually checked out every vehicle that came by. A little blue station wagon went past on the other side of the road and I noticed that the driver and passenger were two girls who seemed to be watching me. I turned my head in interest and watched as they pulled into a parking area, turned around, and drove back, pulling up beside me. The driver, a cute, red-haired girl, asked me if I was heading to Vancouver. I said I was and then she asked if I wanted some company.

Wanted a cute red-haired girl for company??? You know how in the Peanuts cartoon Charlie Brown always dreams about a little red-haired girl? The Charlie Brown in my brain was doing backflips! What unbelievable good luck! Then my brain, which now was functioning at light speed, had doubts. Maybe I had misheard? Maybe I was hallucinating? Fortunately, my mouth, which was evidently running on autopilot, replied that it sounded good to me and said that some company would be fine.

Instead of telling me it was April fool's Day, or that she was actually wanting to know directions, which is what my Charlie Brown brain was expecting, she said that because it was getting late and she had to pack some stuff, that we should go back to Canmore to their cabin and would leave in the morning. And so I found myself in the back of "Victor" the Vauxhall station wagon heading to a little cabin in Canmore. Yippee!

Thieves

Planning to camp at Tunnel Mountain campground, we wished our Canmore friends well and set off in the late afternoon for Banff.

Banff has always been a favourite destination and it did not disappoint us. We checked in at the Tunnel Mountain campground and found a great spot to set up. We had a pair of plastic lawn chairs that had been strapped to the back of the Marmot van ever since we left home. To show that our campsite was occupied, we left the two chairs by the fire pit and climbed into the van to see some sights.

Our first stop was in town at the info centre, where we crowded in with all the other tourists to collect some maps and ask a few questions about what was open and the hours that were kept. We were planning to go to the top of Sulfur Mountain and wanted to know about the gondola ride. We got a good tip to go early to avoid the lineups. We decided that it would be our first activity for the following day. We bought a few groceries and headed back to the campsite.

When we got back to our spot, our chairs were gone. It was pretty disappointing. From one coast to another we had packed those plastic chairs and they were kind of like travelling friends. Not that they were worth much money; they were the kind of chairs that get faded by the sun and eventually get relegated to the back of the shed. But, at that moment, their loss was quite annoying. I even scouted around a bit in hopes of finding them, but no luck. However, if that was the worst thing that was going to happen to us, then we were going to be okay.

We spent quite a while on top of Sulphur Mountain. I really like that gondola ride because there is no way that a lazoid like me would ever climb that high. We did see some folks hiking up the switchback trail when we were passing over them in our comfy ride, which gave me the idea to pose at the foot of the climb as if I might actually hike up, and pose again triumphantly at the top of the mountain in hopes of fooling someone into thinking I had the wherewithal to actually make the ascent. Unfortunately, nobody who knows me would likely to fall for my ruse.

I understand the exhilaration that mountain climbers talk about as they look around from the top of the world. There is an observation deck in a circle around the top of the building at the terminal of the gondola ride. From there, the happy mountaineer can enjoy the panorama of the Rockies and get a bird's eye view of Banff and the Bow Valley below.

On the lookout there are compass markings and flags where we located the directions and distance to our next destination, Wellington, NZ, 12000 kms to the southwest. But that will have to be another story.

Parks Canada tells us:

Located at the top of Sulphur Mountain, the cosmic ray station was completed by the National Research Council in 1956, in preparation for International Geophysical Year (IGY, 1957-1958), an undertaking involving 66 countries and a dozen scientific disciplines. The study of cosmic rays held a prominent place, with 99 cosmic ray stations (nine in Canada) in operation world-wide during IGY. Due to its high elevation, Sulphur Mountain was the most important Canadian station. In 1960, the University of Alberta at Calgary took over the station, which was closed in 1978. The building itself was dismantled in 1981.

The cosmic ray station was not the first scientific facility to be built on Sulphur Mountain. In 1903, a meteorological observatory was completed on nearby Sanson Peak, named in honour of Norman Bethune Sanson, the observer who tended the recording equipment for nearly 30 years. Sanson was in charge of the weather station on Sanson Peak, built there at his suggestion in 1903. He was the curator of the Banff Park Museum from 1896 to 1932.

The peak was named in his honour in 1948. Sanson made more than 1000 trips each one taking 4 hours to reach the peak in his capacity as park meteorologist until 1945, when he was 84 years old.

Eventually, we were sated with alpine wonders and had enough cosmic rays, so we climbed aboard our gondola for the descent. (If you hike all the way up they do not require a ticket to go down.) The first bit, where you leave the building the cable goes from horizontal past a big wheel to what feels like a vertical drop. The gondola plunges down the side of the mountain and provides a great thrill to finish up the visit to the summit.

We hopped into the Marmot van and drove down into the townsite to spend some time poking around in rock and gem shops and the usual tourist traps. We picked up some souvenirs and then headed to the pool. The building is pretty old, but a soak in the pool can be quite comforting. It is best to visit in the off season because it can get pretty crowded.

For those who like a bit more history, a visit to the Cave and Basin National Historic Site is well worth it. I believe their pools are no longer open for bathers, but you can get quite an interesting look at how the place developed and even learn some surprising facts about internment camps.

Skookumchuck?

Back at the campsite, we planned our next adventure. We decided to tour south through the Rockies to Radium Hot Springs, and then visit some friends at Skookumchuck, which is really a tiny dot on the highway. The highway looked like it was not a secondary road, which was good because by now we were pretty shy about travelling poor roads.

The road from Banff to Radium along Highway 93 was the most beautiful and interesting bit of road of our whole trip. You take the Trans-Canada Highway northwest out of Canmore to a place called Castle Mountain Junction, which, as the name implies, is the junction of highways. Highway 93 travels west and south through Vermillion Pass. At the highest point, you cross the border between Alberta and British Columbia and the dividing line between Banff and Kootenay national parks. About half an hour from Banff, there is a pullout off the highway where you can visit a little information stop. There you can see the explanation of the term "continental divide." From that point, all the rivers flow either to the west, joining up with others to ultimately empty into the Pacific Ocean, or to the east, ultimately to empty either into the Gulf of Mexico or into the Atlantic Ocean.

This was the first of many great places to stop and enjoy the mountains and rivers and lakes, so we drove at a leisurely pace and stopped quite often to see the sights. We took advantage of the opportunity to take lots of great photographs and a chance to let Smarmy the Marmot pose for the camera.

To top off this really great scenic highway, you pass through Sinclair Canyon a few miles before you reach Radium. The palisade of rough stone cliffs of Sinclair Canyon looms over both sides of the highway. If you pull off onto the overlook, you get a chance to really take in the wonder of the place. Tiny fir trees somehow manage to cling to the smattering of soil on the canyon ledges, and splashing water tumbles over the rocks below the roadway. From the overlook, a sidewalk leads to another scenic wonder, Redwall Fault, the only bright-red cliffs we have seen in the Canadian Rockies. Out of the canyon, but before you get to the town, you will drive by the hotsprings. The Parks Canada website tells us the history of the place:

In 1890, Roland Stuart paid $1 an acre to receive a Crown grant for the 160 acres surrounding the pool. He expected to reap his rewards from sales of bottled water, but not from bathers. In 1911, a British medical journal suggested that there might be radium in the water. Research by McGill University in 1913 showed this to be true. Stuart realized that his slightly radioactive spring water might have more curative power than the famous springs at Bath, England. He opened a bathing pool and built a bathhouse. The Canadian government expropriated the springs in 1922. Currently, the hotsprings provide all that visitors have come to expect in a modern facility. There are now food and gift concessions in the lobby, as well as a new 4,000 square foot day spa that restores the historic spa services and offers a wide variety of treatment options to patrons.

Although we usually stop to relax in the hot springs, we decided to carry on further south on Highway 95 to Skookumchuck before the day was too far gone. Our friends do not live in downtown Skookumchuck, which is a good thing because one would have to hunt pretty hard to find downtown Skookumchuck. In fact, I would be very surprised if there is such a thing as a downtown. I am told that the greatest municipal debate in Skookumchuck is whether the town's name is spelled *Skookumchuk* or *Skookumchuck*. Either way, the post office is closed down and the mail is delivered to another place altogether.

There is no hustle and bustle of town life when you see their cabin on a rise above the lake. You can walk down through the field to visit the water, or you can sit on the porch and admire the view across the valley to the nearby mountains. This was a great place to relax and enjoy the company of old friends. But, as we found out in conversation, sometimes, like when a bear wandered onto the porch and gave them a good fright, the place is not calm and quiet. We took a good look around before we headed for bed in the Marmot van, which was parked near the porch. Happily, the only sounds we heard as we drifted off to sleep were the calls of the loons.

The next morning, we were back on the road, retracing our route north on Highway 95. We had decided that because we'd taken the southern route through British Columbia on our journey east, we would take the Trans-Canada on our way back west. So we went north through the Columbia Valley.

The Columbia and Kootenay rivers flow through the valley in opposite directions. The Kootenay actually starts a little farther north in an adjoining valley and flows south past Canal Flats where it passes within 2 km of Columbia Lake , the source of the Columbia River which flows north. Both rivers wind their way through mountain valleys before joining together 700 kilometres later at Castelgar B.C. Centered between the Rockies to the east and Purcells on the west, this valley is also known as the "Warmer Side of the Canadian Rockies." The area is famous for its tourism amenities, such as world class skiing, golfing, natural hot springs, and abundant wildlife.

We toured through Canal Flats, Windermere, and Invermere, past Radium again, then Edgewater, Spillimacheen, and Parson, and joined the Trans-Canada at Golden, where we stopped to have our lunch.

Golden is about three-quarters of an hour west of Field, which we had bypassed by taking the side trip to Skookumchuck. However, I will take you on a little trip back in time and space, to Field.

Falling in the Mountains

The red-haired girl and I arrived in Field the day after she and her friend had taken me to the cabin in Canmore. That cabin was delightfully rustic, nestled among the trees on a wooded lot at the edge of town. The path to the front door wound through the trees where I noticed a little feeder fixed to the side of a tree which was where "Squirrely" came for treats. Inside the cabin, there was a wood stove for heat and cooking, and a hand pump on the counter for water.

I found out later that the woodstove provided a bit of a test. The usual procedure when leaving the cabin was to be sure to split kindling for the next visitors and to fill the wood box with firewood. The girls asked me if I would look after the kindling and firewood while they made some supper. Being cabin veterans who had grown up in the city, they were proud of their woodcutting skills and wanted to know how I might measure up.

One might think that kindling is used only to start a fire, but in my experience, kindling was a useful tool to be used all day long. I had grown up in a house where the only cooking and heating was done with a woodstove. My mother was an excellent cook and fed a large family. That meant she had to be a master of the dark art of woodstove temperature control. There were no dials on the woodstove to set the temperature; no high, low, or medium, only a rough system of drafts and damper. This meant that the cook had to practice a certain kind of black magic to keep the fire at just the right level for the job.

The main ingredient in that black magic was kindling. If the fire was a little bit slow, a handful of kindling quickly brought the temperature up to the desired heat. She used lots and lots of kindling, boxfuls and boxfuls and boxfuls. For many years, I was a slave to that kindling box. I could never pass that woodstove without the dread of seeing the exposed bottom of the empty kindling box. So being an old hand I had the firewood done in a blink. Who knew that wood chopping skills would impress girls?

The supper was great, and we sat around talking for a while, making a plan to get a ride in "Victor" the next morning as far as Lake Louise, where we would begin hitchhiking to the west coast. With a full stomach and a cozy cabin, I was feeling pretty drowsy. The bus ride I had taken from Brandon to Calgary was quite a long one, maybe 18 hours or so, and I had not slept much, so I was happy to roll out my sleeping bag in the living room and have an early night.

The next morning, the red-haired girl and I found ourselves standing at the side of the highway outside Lake Louise watching Victor disappear back to Canmore. That day was a good news-bad news kind of day. First the bad news: getting a ride anywhere near Banff was pretty tough. It ranked right up there with Brandon and Wawa. All day on the side of the road and we managed to travel 27 kilometers to Field. The good news was that my travelling companion made the beauty of the scenery pale in comparison. I can think of nothing on my journey that was more pleasant than to spend the day getting to know that pretty girl who seemed quite happy to be getting to know me. The only downside was that she was not very impressed with the lunch I provided, which was my favourite travelling food — cheese and buns.

Golden

Golden started as a pretty routine stop for us. We filled the fuel tanks and looked around for a spot to have a picnic lunch. We found a place to park the Marmot van close by the river and had a bit of lunch. After we had eaten, we felt like stretching our legs a bit and, noticing a trail that wound its way along the side of the river, we decided to do a bit of exploring. It turned out to be a very interesting little jaunt. The highlight was when we came to the Kicking Horse River Pedestrian Bridge.

Evidently, it's the longest freestanding timber frame bridge in Canada. It is 151 feet long – that's 46 m for those of you of the metric persuasion. Planned as a community event in 2001, over 100 members of the Timber Framers Guild came from the U.S.A., Europe, and all over Canada to help build and raise the bridge. It weighs approximately 210,000 lbs. and was constructed of 72,000 board feet of Douglas-fir timbers. It's a stunning piece of intricate architecture and definitely worth a look.

It was very hot by the time we reached our penultimate stop, Revelstoke. We had grown tired of the joys of trying to sleep in a very hot camper, so we took a motel room and cranked up the air conditioner. The bonus was that our motel was nowhere near any railway tracks.

After stealth camping in Nelson B.C., we were understandably shy about trying to sleep while all the trains in North America thundered past. One look at all the train tracks in Revelstoke made us shudder.

The Wikipedia article about Revelstoke contains the marvel of understatement:

Revelstoke's economy has traditionally been tied to the Canadian Pacific Railway (CPR) and it still maintains a strong connection to that industry. A strong connection? If you like trains, Revelstoke has trains. There are lots and lots of trains and they are very easy to track down. Tracks are everywhere. You can see trains, you can hear trains, and if you are close enough, you can even smell trains! You must visit the railway museum.

The Revelstoke Railway Museum presents the history of the Canadian Pacific Railway in the Columbia Mountains, as well as the role the railway, and its workers, have played in building Canada as a nation. A large collection of artifacts, historical photographs, artwork, and full-sized rolling stock are displayed, including a steam locomotive built for mountain work.

The architecture of the museum was designed to resemble a rail yard with a stylized version of a water tower. It's a significant landmark on Track Street at Victoria Road in downtown Revelstoke. Three exhibit galleries are complemented by outdoor rolling stock displays as well as audio-visual presentations and a children's caboose play area.

But as I said we had enough of trains so we were back on the highway and left the railyards behind. The road from Revelstoke to Kamloops is quite a challenging piece of the Trans-Canada. The highway winds through the mountain valleys and there is a lot of truck traffic. It's only two lanes in places, which makes it difficult for vehicles to overtake and pass one another. A couple of times we found ourselves crowded from behind by drivers who wanted to go more quickly than we did, and hindered by vehicles that wanted to travel more slowly than we.

Happily, the highway improved as we approached Kamloops but the weather was hot! Too hot! We decided to have an early day of it, so instead of driving any further we gave into the dark side once more and found a hotel to cool down and spend the night. It was a very good decision.

The following morning, we set out early to beat the heat. It wasn't long before we were no longer Beyond Hope. We were almost home. One last observation from my hitchhiking trip came to mind as we were passing by Hope.

My red-haired travelling partner and I had caught a ride from Kamloops with a middle-aged fellow driving a truck with a camper. He was very obliging and opened the back door of the camper so we could stow our gear and then the three of us settled in on the big bench seat in the cab. Those old pickup trucks were built for three people in the cab, so we had plenty of room, although I have been told that the reason cowboys have their hats curled up on the sides is so they can fit three in a pickup.

At first the driver introduced himself to us and we did likewise. Then he regaled us with a description of the pleasant holiday he was returning from. As he told us about the past few weeks he'd spent fishing various lakes in the north Okanagan area, we could tell he had really enjoyed his vacation. The fishing had been fun he told us, but just getting away from day-to-day life was really what he enjoyed the most. He talked about how much he enjoyed his camper and his vacation cooking had been a pleasure.

He bought us a coffee and donut in Hope and remarked as we got back in the truck that just a couple of hours more and we would be in Vancouver. As we travelled toward the coast, the traffic increased and the mountain scenery changed to farms and towns. As the landscape changed, so did our driver's demeanour. He began to talk about his business and the jobs that waited him once he got home. He began to get a bit touchy about the traffic and his good humour and relaxed attitude began to fade away. By the time he let us out in the city, we could tell he was feeling a bit pressed; although he was still pleasant to us, he was cursing at the traffic. The change in environment had clearly made a change in his disposition. After we got out and waved him goodbye, we talked about the change he had undergone. My wish is that he retired to those fishing lakes where he seemed so happy with life.

Home Again

Back home on our island that night, we were glad to be in our own bed. We had unpacking and laundry and sifting through souvenirs, and the half ton of "interesting rocks" that Donna had picked up. But we could take care of that over the next few days.

We also had to get back into thinking about the day-to-day cares and chores. There was the unread mail to go through and sort and a million other things to fill up our days. All too soon we were back into a routine at home. Within a couple of months we were aboard a ship headed across the Pacific for New Zealand and so it took some time before I began to think about writing this book.

It had been a wonderful trip – 2 1/2 months and 15,000 kilometers. Of course there were a few bumps in the road here and there. Writing gave me a chance to relive some memories. It was a delight to have some fun with the geography and the people we encountered along the way, and to spin a few yarns about my youth.

Reflecting on our travels has fostered another of my many theories. This one is about the perception of time.

Many, many, months have passed during my working life which have compressed into vague memories in my mind, but the time spent going to new places and doing new things tends to stretch out time and paint vivid memories. It is like an ordinary day in adult life which can flip by hardly noticed, compared to a day in the life of a child when the world is all new and stretches out, full of wonders.

I can still remember almost every day of that hitchhiking trip so many years ago and this latest road trip has been packed with days of marvellous new memories. My theory, in a nutshell: *Day to day time tends to shrink and time in new places and with new people stretches.* So, in accordance with my theory, I want to keep on travelling and stretch out the time I have left.

End

Detail of a bench carving in Hope, B.C.
(Pete Ryan -carver)

Smarmy, our mascot, makes new friends at Manning Park.

Hedley B.C. Museum After the billions of dollars of gold and silver were removed.
Photo courtesy of OurBC

Drumheller
with
dinosaurs,
hoodoos,
fossils and
fun.

Ukrainian history comes alive near Mundare, Alberta.

A sod house. Western Development Museum Saskatoon.

Unusual sights on the prairies: an Easter egg in the sky in Vegreville, and a blue buffalo in a clear box in Mundare.

A viking and a fisherman
pose in Gimli Manitoba.

Duct tape- a
desperate
attempt to keep
the Ontario
bugs out of the

Lester Pearson holds a
pet marmot.
Parliament Buildings
Ottawa

Goderich,
Ontario–The
gaol where
they might
have had a
cell for me
in 1970.

Photos courtesy
of Huron County
Museum and
Historic Gaol

Me helping the pilot hop the fence to get
onto his ship. Welland Canal

The Famous Wawa Goose. Photo: Municipality of Wawa

The lesser known Wawa Pickle Barrel.

Smarmy and Charlotte honeymooning at Niagara

Smarmy's cousin Wiarton Willie.

Funny signs in Quebec

The Three Musketeers - Fortress Louisbourg, N.S.

The fourth musketeer demonstrating her weapon and posing with her new buddy.

The Hector brought the first Scots to Nova Scotia. It was a terrible trip on a dreadful ship.

High Tide Low Tide - Walking the ocean

A cooper making barrels at Ross Farm, Nova Scotia.

oops!

Me at the longest covered bridge in the world.

1282 feet long.

Do ye see any lobster there, Billy?

Shediac, N.B.

The Giant Axe in Nackawic, New Brunswick

Banff

The ride up Sulfur Mountain in the gondola.

Mountain climbing made easy.

The scary bit when you suddenly drop over the side of the mountain.

Acknowledgements

This is where I have to take responsibility for all the errors and irritations you might find in this book, especially if you are a Nakuspidore or Canmoron or a Muskievite. I also owe a lot of people my gratitude.

First, I want to thank my friends and family, who provided support, talked things over, read, offered comments, and gave their time when I asked. You know who you are.

Next, I want to acknowledge in particular Bob Collins for his advice and his example.

Maggie Paquet, my editor deserves my thanks as well for helping me through this process.

Most importantly, I want to thank my wife and travelmate Donna who puts up with my theories and bad jokes and keeps me from losing my focus.

About the Author

Ralph began writing at the age of 8 and at that time Mrs. Klemanski reported, "Ralph's writing is quite messy and it is hardly more legible than his awkward printing. Perhaps he would do well to consider a career as a doctor."

Undaunted, he continued to write throughout his childhood and into his adult life. Despite his abominable penmanship Ralph's work has actually been published in newspapers and magazines. This is his first book for grown-ups.

In 1959 Ralph moved with his family to Vancouver Island and has mostly lived there since. He and his wife now live in Qualicum Beach. He started going to school in 1958 and continued until 2008. Since he retired he enjoys writing, travelling, old cars, and old motorcycles.

Printed in Great Britain
by Amazon

52404110R00123